We Live the Good Life

Growing Spiritually through the *Catechism of the Catholic Church*

Part Three: The Moral Life

Deacon Henry Libersat

Pauline
BOOKS & MEDIA
Boston

Imprimatur:
† Norbert M. Dorsey, C.P.
Bishop of Orlando
January 22, 1997

Library of Congress Cataloging-in-Publication Data

Libersat, Henry.
  We live the good life : growing spiritually through the Catechism of the Catholic Church / Henry Libersat.
     p. cm. — (A Catholic confession of faith)
  ISBN 0-8198-8290-9 (pbk.)
  1. Catholic Church. Catechismus Ecclesiae Catholicæ. 2. Spiritual life—Catholic Church. 3. Catholic Church—Catechisms. I. Title. II. Series: Libersat, Henry. Catholic confession of faith.
BX1959.5.L53   1997
241'.042—dc21   196-50957
                                                                                   CIP

The Scripture quotations contained herein are from the *New Revised Standard Version Bible: Catholic Edition,* copyright © 1996 and 1989 by the Division of Christian Education of the National Council of Churches of Christ in the U.S.A. Used by permission. All rights reserved.

English translation of the *Catechism of the Catholic Church* for the United States of America copyright © 1994, United States Catholic Conference, Inc.—Libreria Editrice Vaticana. Used with permission.

Copyright © 1997, Henry Libersat

Printed and published in the U.S.A. by Pauline Books & Media, 50 St. Paul's Avenue, Boston, MA 02130.

http://www.pauline.org

E-mail: PBM_EDIT@INTERRAMP.COM

Pauline Books & Media is the publishing house of the Daughters of St. Paul, an international congregation of women religious serving the Church with the communications media.

Thanks and Dedication

In a small country cemetery between Henry, Louisiana and Erath, Louisiana, lie the remains of my father and mother, Henry (Sr.) and Elda Libersat. Nearby lie Pierre and Olive, my paternal grandparents. Other relatives are buried there and in another country cemetery in Bancker, Louisiana. Still others lie in Texas and Florida, for example, my maternal grandparents, Clay and Cora Zeringue.

These relatives have been a great part of my life, even since their death. They all loved me and cared for me in so many different ways. They were all Catholic and lived the faith as best they could, given their understanding of it. They all knew and loved God.

I want to dedicate *A Catholic Confession of Faith,* to them all. This "work" is actually four small books, *We Believe, We Celebrate the Mystery, We Live the Good Life,* and *We Pray.*

But in a very special way, these four books are dedicated to the memory of my wonderful parents, whose love for God and the Church gave me the foundation for my life as husband, father and grandfather, as well as for my recent decade of ministry in the Catholic Church as a deacon and for my nearly four decades of service in the Catholic press.

Thanks, Mom. Thanks, Dad.

Thanks, too, to those many priests, sisters and faithful laity whose example, love and encouragement have kept me trying to live the good life.

Truly, I am grateful to the bishop-publishers of *The Florida Catholic* for the opportunity to serve God and the Church through that interdiocesan publishing venture. I am grateful for their trust and pastoral guidance.

I am also grateful to the Daughters of St. Paul for their confidence in me and for their encouragement in my extra-curricular writing. This series brings to six the number of books I have written for Pauline Books & Media. The first two, *Way, Truth and Life* and *Do Whatever He Tells You* are presentations of our Catholic faith from a perspective of daily life. They are rooted in doctrine, Scripture and prayer, but are written in a more popular style. While I have tried to use real-life stories in this series, the books here are a bit more formal in presentation and more directly concerned with Church teaching as presented in the *Catechism of the Catholic Church*.

Given the reader response to the material as it was presented in *The Florida Catholic*, I have high hopes that these books will help many other readers. In series form in the newspaper, the material was used by many people in religious education, Re-Membering Church and RCIA, as well as for personal reflection.

Contents

CHAPTER 1
The Call to Be Fully Alive 15

CHAPTER 2
Be Good with the Goodness of God 21

CHAPTER 3
What Does It Mean to Be Free? 25

CHAPTER 4
Anatomy of a Moral Act 31

CHAPTER 5
What Makes a Conscience Moral? 37

CHAPTER 6
What Are Virtues? How Do We Become Virtuous? 43

CHAPTER 7
Natural Goodness and Grace 47

CHAPTER 8
The Truth about Sin 53

CHAPTER 9
The Truth about Mercy 59

CHAPTER 10
Morality and Society 63

Chapter 11
Authority and the Common Good 69

Chapter 12
The Moral Law: What Is It? 75

Chapter 13
Old Law and Gospel Law 81

Chapter 14
To Be Justified by Grace 85

Chapter 15
The Church, Mother and Teacher 91

Chapter 16
A Look at the Ten Commandments 97

Chapter 17
Our Relationship with God 101

Chapter 18
Our Relationship with God:
The Second and Third Commandments 107

Chapter 19
Our Relationship with Our Neighbors 113

Chapter 20
You Shall Not Kill 119

Chapter 21
Sexual Fidelity: In Spirit and in Deed 125

Chapter 22
Don't Even Want What Your Neighbor Has! ... 131

Chapter 23
Do Not Lie about Your Neighbor 137

About *A Catholic Confession of Faith*...

I thought I was "riding high" when Pauline Books & Media agreed to print a revision of two series of articles in book form. *We Believe* and *We Celebrate the Mystery* had already been published in *The Florida Catholic*. I had done what I started out to do. Honestly, I thought I was "written out" for at least another few months.

When Sister Mary Mark of Pauline Books & Media mentioned yet two more books, one on morality and one on prayer, I inwardly gulped but immediately said, "Yes, I will be happy to do them!" I gulped because I realized the amount of work I was taking on. But I immediately agreed to do the two other books for three good reasons.

First, it was a good idea and one I would share first of all with readers of *The Florida Catholic*. This statewide Catholic newspaper is my first professional love. Second, it seemed the Holy Spirit was talking to the Sisters: *We Believe* shared the content of our faith; *We Celebrate the Mystery* spoke of the awesome and loving presence of God in our sacramental life. Now, We Live the Good Life will help people refocus on how we respond to God's great love, and *We Pray* will discuss the wonderful ways God invites us into a personal relationship with him. Third, I realized I must personally revisit my own response to God's love,

A Catholic Confession of Faith

and the *Catechism of the Catholic Church* would be a wonderful aid in this task. Doing the books would make me do what I needed to do.

Each chapter in these four books ends with a reflection which will hopefully help individuals and groups to think about and discuss the material presented.

It is my prayer that all readers will benefit in reading *A Catholic Confession of Faith* as I did in writing them. The work was a joy; the response to the work was a blessing. May it give glory to God who is Father, Son and Spirit!

Deacon Henry Libersat
Pentecost, 1996

We Live the Good Life
About This Book...

Everybody wants to be happy, to live the good life. For one person, happiness means owning the best set of golf clubs and shooting under ninety. For another, living the good life means being the most popular girl in school or owning the most luxurious house in town. For still another, it means marrying the most beautiful woman or the most handsome man, or wielding great financial and political power. People seek happiness with a passion—and sometimes human passions are mistaken for joy and happiness.

But if possessions or human passions lead to happiness, why are so many rich people and passionate people so unhappy and so frantically searching for happiness?

Happiness itself pales in the face of true joy. Joy is that sense of well-being, of peacefulness that comes from loving oneself enough to seek what is truly best. What is best for each of us is to become truly human, to become what our God intended us to be, holy images of himself.

The Church insistently calls us to seek the greater good and to put sin aside. People may think the Church is outdated, that sin is not so bad after all and makes people happy. But sin does not make people happy. We are created in God's image; we are his people, the sheep of his flock. We can never find peace of mind and joy of spirit unless we become one with God in mind and in spirit. That is the secret to true happiness, the kind of happiness we spell j-o-y.

Bishop Norbert M. Dorsey, CP, trustee of the partnership of bishop-publishers of *The Florida Catholic,* graciously gave me permission to redo this material which first appeared as a series in that statewide newspaper. Father Alfred Cioffi of the Archdiocese of Miami was my theological consultant in this material on morality. Both, along with my wife, Peggy, deserve my gratitude. They all share in whatever good these pages may accomplish.

This little book, *We Live the Good Life,* is the third in the series called *A Catholic Confession of Faith.* It is a reflection on morality as presented in the *Catechism of the Catholic Church.* I have tried to use relevant examples from real life to demonstrate the various lessons of each chapter.

If readers, through this work, can understand better that God's commandments and the moral teachings of the Church are intended for our own good, to lead us into the ultimate experience of true freedom and to lead us toward true happiness, it will have served its purpose.

Deacon Henry Libersat
All Souls, 1996

Chapter 1

The Call to Be Fully Alive

A businessman who sells shoes faces a serious decision: find a way to increase income, or lay off employees. He could buy quality shoes from a manufacturer, but only at high prices, since he cannot buy in volume as do his larger competitors. He could buy a lesser quality shoe, use a slick advertising program to make them seem better than they are, and charge more. In that way, he can make enough money to keep his employees on the payroll. What to do?

• A high school student needs to earn a scholarship to continue her education. She needs to have a 4.0 average to outdo another student who is also competing for the same scholarship. The first student comes from a very poor family and she needs that scholarship to finance her education. Without it, she may well have to drag out her schooling for six or eight years as she works longer hours to make ends meet. Another student offers her a stolen copy of the test questions and answers. What to do?

• A model faces a serious choice. The head of a major modeling firm wants to hire him to model fashions at home in America and in Europe. It's the chance of a lifetime; he's been working hard for just such a break. With this new job, he may well end up on the cover of major fashion magazines. It could help him break into the acting career he yearns for, but there is one problem. Although this job could help him provide his wife and two children with a much better life, it would take him away from home for long periods of time. His wife opposes the move. They are deeply in debt. What to do?

Life is full of decisions, many of which involve serious concerns. Decisions can be right or wrong, moral or immoral. What makes something right or wrong? To what or to whom do people turn to help decide what they should do in a particular circumstance? Can't people simply do what they *feel* is right? What is conscience and what guides it? How do I know I can trust my conscience?

In this book, we will look at these questions. But first, let's review the preceding two books on material from the *Catechism of the Catholic Church: We Believe* and *We Celebrate the Mystery*. In *We Believe,* we discussed our faith (what is revealed and what we believe). In *We Celebrate the Mystery,* we examined our encounter with God in the seven sacraments of the Church. Here is a synopsis of the content of those two books.

God has no beginning nor end. God always was, is now and always will be. There is one God, yet there are three Persons in God: Father, Son and Holy Spirit. Each is fully God, and possesses the fullness of the divine nature.

God created all things; he created Adam and Eve. They were sinless, but they chose to sin and their sin disrupted their relationship with God and all creation. Since that first sin, human nature has been damaged. It is weak and inclined toward sin. But God promised a Savior: Jesus Christ, the Son of God, true God and true man. Jesus died on the cross and offered himself as a sacrifice for us.

He took our sins unto himself. He was both priest and victim of that once-for-all sacrifice which redeems human nature and reconciles us with God if we accept Jesus as our Lord and Savior.

Jesus founded the Church, which celebrates the redemptive life, death and resurrection of Jesus in the liturgy. Through participation in the sacraments we become members of the Church, the Body of Christ. We receive the Holy Spirit and are forgiven our personal sins. We are blessed indeed to receive in Holy Communion the Body and Blood of Jesus Christ. At Mass, the grace of God makes us present at the one sacrifice that took place on Calvary. Some of us are set aside by Holy Orders to serve the rest of the Christian community. Many of us are married and have become true sacramental signs of God's love in the world. When we are sick, we are anointed with holy oil and benefit from the prayers of the Church.

Christ is the head of the Church, which has his authority to preach the Gospel and to teach its members what is right and what is wrong. The Church is led by the Pope and the bishops in communion with him. They have custody of the Scriptures and under the power of the Holy Spirit authentically interpret the Word of God for the faithful. They teach with authority what God says is moral and immoral in human thought and conduct, and in matters of faith and doctrine, what is true and what is untrue.

Now let's return to the examples of the businessman, model and student. Each of them stands to lose or gain much depending on his or her decision. Sometimes a person may believe that doing something that seems wrong may be good because it serves a good end. It would be good to keep employees on the payroll, but is it moral to do so at the expense of an injustice to customers? The student's desire for a good education is laudable, but is cheating and unfairly edging out her competition for a scholarship the right and moral thing to do? The male model has a good goal, to provide for his family, but his wife has serious reservations. She may fear that separation will weaken the marriage and the children may suffer from the long absences of their father. More money and a good break in his career are indeed good goals, but the moral dilemma is evident.

What does a person need to know to make a good moral decision, one that will, because it is *right,* mean peace of mind and more happiness in the long run? First of all, there can be a vast difference between what is *legal* (the law of the land), what is *ethical* (in professions and cultures) and what is *moral.* For the Christian, morality is based on natural law. The *Catechism of the Catholic Church* states that law "is a rule of conduct enacted by competent authority for the sake of the common good" (no. 1951). The natural law "expresses the original moral sense which enables man to discern by reason the good and the evil, the truth and the lie." Quoting Pope Leo XIII, the *Catechism* states: "The natural law is written and engraved in the soul of each and every man, because it is human reason ordaining him to do good and forbidding him to sin.... But this command of human reason would not have the force of law if it were not the voice and interpreter of a higher reason to which our spirit and our freedom must be submitted" (no. 1954).

In other words, human reason and a good conscience can recognize right and wrong by submission to God who is Creator and who has instilled in us the ability to recognize his will and his way. God created us "to know him, to love him and to serve him in this life and to be happy with him forever in heaven." That's what most

Catholics have learned from their early childhood. God knows what is best for us and wants that for us. He shares with us his own divine life, his joy, peace and eternal happiness. Even now, in this life, through grace, we can experience God's happiness and blessedness—in a word, his *beatitude*.

Reflection:

- Privately reflect on a past major moral decision you had to resolve.

    a) How did you resolve the problem?

    b) How important were the Ten Commandments and Church teaching in your deliberations?

- Would you respond to the challenge differently to day? If so, why and how?
- Discuss with a friend a major moral issue in your community.

    a) What values are involved?

    b) How do the Ten Commandments shed light on the problem?

CHAPTER 2

Be Good with the Goodness of God

Holiness *is* the good life—not a limitation on life. Holy persons are *wholesome*. They have peace of mind, even when things go badly, or even after personal sin, because they see the whole picture.

Holy persons seek to balance responsibility for others with personal needs and recognize what is good and bad in life's situations and choices. Three examples quickly come to mind.

1. Holy persons enjoy food, but they eat to live and do not live to eat. An over-abundance of food in my pantry means I have something that belongs to others. I *owe* that abundance to those who have little or nothing to eat. Hoarding food is as sinful as hoarding money. Holy persons share with the needy and help them overcome their limitations.

2. Holy persons esteem the gift of sexuality, but sexual passion does not run their lives. Sexual intercourse becomes the expression of total commitment to one's husband or wife, and that mutual and exclusive commitment makes sexual pleasure all the more glorious. Fidelity to oneself and one's spouse adds meaning and proclaims the dignity of both man and wife. Lust is not the language of love. Love builds up and never tears down another

person. Love never takes advantage or oppresses. Love heals and never wounds. St. Paul put it so powerfully:

> Love is patient; love is kind; love is not envious or boastful or arrogant or rude. It does not insist on its own way; it is not irritable or resentful; it does not rejoice in wrongdoing, but rejoices in the truth. It bears all things, believes all things, hopes all things, endures all things (1 Cor 13:4-7).

3. When insulted, holy persons may indeed feel anger but do not as a rule fly into a rage or try to hurt the other person in return. If I am holy, or trying to be holy, I want to understand what provoked the insult. Was it the result of a real or imagined slight? Was it related to someone else entirely and I just happened to be in the way? Have I hurt others and now understand better how they felt?

Holy persons do not always live up to the ideal Christian way of life. But they recognize when they have not, and they repent and make amends, striving to do better. It isn't easy to be holy, but it isn't impossible. One person said that to be holy is "to be good with the goodness of God." God's goodness is the source and foundation of all holiness. In calling us to holiness, God does not call us to the impossible. With God all things are possible.

Holiness is so precious that the *Catechism of the Catholic Church,* early in its treatment of morality, calls Christians especially to cling to the life given them in Baptism. The *Catechism* quotes St. Leo the Great:

> Christians, recognize your dignity and, now that you share in God's own nature, do not return to your former base condition by sinning. Remember who is your head and of whose body you are a member. Never forget that you have been rescued from the power of darkness and brought into the light of the kingdom of God (no.1691).

In the Sermon on the Mount, Jesus' beatitudes "purify our hearts in order to teach us to love God above all things" (no. 1728). We "love God above all things" when we make the right moral choices in response to challenges. One basic challenge is to remember that although you have sinned, God is calling you to repentance and a life of perfection. The fundamental correct choice is to obey God. Here are three examples of how that choice may be expressed:

1. If I am consumed with the desire to eat for the sheer pleasure of eating, I will seek help and ask God to heal me of this condition. I will make a conscious decision to share food with the hungry.

2. If I seem to be obsessed with sexual desires and fantasies, I will seek forgiveness in confession and help through counseling; I will make a daily commitment to see myself and others as images of God who deserve both reverence and respect. A man once told a friend, "When I find myself lusting after a woman, I try to remember to pray: 'Lord, thank you for such beauty. Protect this woman from all harm and from the feelings I have in my heart right now.'"

3. If I have a tendency to want to get even when I am offended, I will seek spiritual direction, confess my anger as needed and offer my pain to God as a forgiving prayer for those who hurt me. I will ask forgiveness of those whom I have hurt.

Some of the above ideas are rooted in a wonderful book, *Jesus' Pattern for a Happy Life: The Beatitudes,* published by Liguori Books. The author, Marilyn Gustin, took each beatitude from the Sermon on the Mount and gave true examples of how some people live them out. She explained how to develop the habit of opting for the values in the beatitudes. She believed that to be virtuous, one must practice virtue and she provided spiritual exercises to develop a virtuous life. Good reading!

The beatitudes are part of Jesus' response to the desire for happiness "that God has placed in the human heart." They teach us the "final end to which God calls us: the Kingdom, the vision of God, participation in the divine nature, eternal life, filiation, rest in God." The beatitudes "confront us with decisive choices concerning earthly goods; they purify our hearts in order to teach us to love God above all things." The beatitude (blessing) of heaven "sets the standards for discernment in the use of earthly goods in keeping with the law of God" (nos. 1725-1729).

Reflection:

- Read Matthew 5:3-11. Describe how each beatitude reflects the goodness of God.
- Are the three examples about changing bad habits practical? Can you suggest other examples?

Chapter 3

What Does It Mean to Be Free?

A woman was asked, "What does it mean to be free?" She said, "Call George."

Her husband George had been in prison for three years. The couple had been struggling to get a new trial or a resentencing hearing. Even the prosecuting attorney was admitting the conviction was a mistake, but federal officials had their own routines. It was hard to get a hearing.

"Ask George." George knew what it meant not to be free, to be unfairly imprisoned. He was separated from home and family. His children were marrying and having babies and he was locked away from them in another state.

"Ask George."

If you asked George, he would tell you that freedom is much more than being out of prison. Freedom has a positive side; it's not just not being locked up. Freedom is being all you can be, doing all you are supposed to do. Freedom is somehow connected with love and celebrating love. George found new meaning to freedom as he whiled away month after month in prison.

Many people thought Pope John Paul II was wasting his time when he wrote an encyclical on morality. But *Splendor of Truth,* published in 1994, hit home on the important issue of human freedom. The Holy Father said that human freedom is irrevocably rooted in who we are as creatures and children of God. Freedom cannot be defined apart from God's will and design for us. We are creatures of God, made in the image of God. We are destined to share that beatitude which is God's own eternal life. Responsibility comes with freedom and part of that responsibility is proper formation of conscience. A properly formed conscience assents to God's commandments and the doctrinal and moral teachings of the Church. A Catholic whose conscience is not in harmony with the teachings of the Church does not have a properly formed conscience.

The *Catechism of the Catholic Church* states:

> God created man a rational being, conferring on him the dignity of a person who can initiate and control his own actions. "God willed that man should be 'left in the hand of his own counsel' so that he might of his own accord seek his Creator and freely attain his full and blessed perfection by cleaving to him" (no. 1730).

If a man or a woman is not seeking God and God's will, that person is not exercising freedom properly. Our destiny, by God's design, is eternal life in him. If we cleave to the sin which springs from our fallen nature, we do not cleave to God and seek our true destiny.

Freedom is power, but it is rooted in reason. It is the power to act or not to act, to choose between different options of belief and conduct, to "perform deliberate actions on one's own responsibility." Our human freedom "is a force for growth and maturity in truth and goodness; it attains its perfection when directed toward God..." (no. 1731).

Sometimes people find the laws of God and the Church oppressive. As one young teenage boy put it, "Why does the Church mess around with our lives? If a girl and I truly love one another, why can't we have sex?" Here, sexual appetite is intensified by youth and novelty, by ignorance of the purpose of human life and of God's love for us as expressed in his holy will. This young man may have chosen to do what "seemed right" and what he undoubtedly wanted to do, without having an adequate understanding of his own human nature. If he made such a choice, he was not acting in true human and moral freedom but was actually undermining his freedom.

> The more one does what is good, the freer one becomes. There is no true freedom except in the service of what is good and just. The choice to disobey and do evil is an abuse of freedom and leads to "the slavery of sin."
>
> Freedom makes man *responsible* for his acts to the extent they are voluntary. Progress in virtue, knowledge of the good, and ascesis [self-discipline] enhance the mastery of the will over its acts (nos. 1733-1734).

Persons are responsible for their own actions to the degree they understand those actions in the light of reason and of God's revealed truths. Personal responsibility for an evil deed, for example, may be lessened or even nullified "by ignorance, inadvertence, duress, fear, habit, inordinate attachments, and other psychological or social factors" (no. 1735).

If our teenager surrenders to his passions and does nothing about his ignorance, he can become enslaved by a sinful way of life. This is not freedom in any true sense of the word. The same danger lurks when anyone makes light of any sin, such as greed, envy, sloth, pride or gluttony.

Pleading ignorance before God and others can be dangerous. If a person is willfully ignorant, any wrongdoing can be considered at least "indirectly voluntary," such as when a traffic accident results from one's refusal to study safe driving rules. The person has been negligent. Consider an even more grave example. A father is handling a loaded pistol and forgets it is loaded. He pulls the trigger and a bullet goes through a wall and kills his child. Negligence has caused a death.

However, when a situation is beyond one's control, one is not considered responsible for what is clearly an evil. For example, it is not right to abuse one's body by overwork and inadequate rest. However, if a mother is "dead on her feet" because she is caring for a critically ill child, there is no guilt. In fact, she is showing heroic virtue and love. On the other hand, if a drunk driver maims or kills someone, he is responsible for his actions because he could reasonably foresee that his intoxication could result in death for himself or another (cf. nos. 1736-1737).

Certain *threats to freedom* exist. Freedom does not mean one can say or do anything one wishes, since a human being is not oriented only to fulfill personal whims and desires. Social and political conditions can hamper the exercise of freedom; by deviating from "moral law man violates his own freedom, becomes imprisoned within himself, disrupts neighborly fellowship, and rebels against divine truth" (no. 1740).

As St. Paul tells us, "For freedom Christ has set us free" (Gal 5:1). We are freed from sin to remain free from sin and to embrace what is good. In Christ we "have communion with the 'truth that makes us free'" (Jn 8:32) and already "we glory in the 'liberty of the children of God'" (Rom 8:21) (no. 1741).

God's will is in no way a "rival" to our desire for true human freedom. Contrary to that notion, we know that God created us with human emotions and appetites.

Those appetites are basically good, but sin has damaged our ability to subdue and order our passions to what is good and moral, or what is the will of God. As the *Catechism* states, we learn, especially from prayer, that the more docile we are before God, the more we respond to the call of grace and the more we grow in true freedom (cf. no. 1742). Here we speak of that inner freedom which enables us to experience confidence in hard times, in temptation and in the face of pressures from a world that ignores or even at times hates the Gospel.

That is the work of the Holy Spirit. He forms in us a spiritual freedom to help us work freely with him in his work in the Church and in the world.

Reflection:

- Meditate quietly on St. Paul's statement, "For freedom Christ has set us free" (Gal 5:1).
    - a) With your spouse or a friend, discuss what this means to you.
    - b) Discuss how we can grow in freedom.
- How does "poverty in spirit" or "being docile before God" help us respond more readily to God's grace?

Chapter 4

Anatomy of a Moral Act

A group of friends was gathered around a picnic table in a state park. One husband said to his friend's wife, "I think you put too much trust in feelings. After all, feelings are neither good nor bad; they just are."

The woman countered, "But feelings are real. We have to deal with them."

A widow remarked, "You bet your life they're real. I'm still furious that Sam died without leaving me sufficient life insurance. It's hard to struggle to make ends meet. We had a good life when he was alive, but now that he's gone, I'm alone and lonely. I feel those things. And I'm mad, too, mad at Sam. I don't want to hurt you, but I'm mad because you two couples have each other and I'm all alone."

Feelings are a very real part of our life, deeply rooted in our human nature. Unlike all the other animals in the world, we operate on reason and not instinct. Our feelings, or passions, take on special significance because we know right from wrong, or, at least, we *can* know right from wrong. We have the freedom to choose to learn or not to learn, to do what is right or to do what is wrong.

If we want to grow in freedom and stature as human beings made in the image of God, we must revisit what goes into moral choices. Three factors go into decisions of moral consequence.

First, there is the *situation* in which we encounter moral dilemmas and are given choices between right and wrong. There are *influences* in each situation. Finally, there are the *circumstances* of the situation. The results of our decisions and actions are considered *consequences* involved in the question.

The widow in our opening story, (whom we'll call Susan), is in a real situation. She is angry with her late husband, Sam, because he did not have more life insurance. She is angry at God and her friends. That's part of the situation in which she finds herself. Some of the influences in that situation are her anger itself, which is a *passion* that must be taken into consideration, and her own responsibility in making decisions with Sam concerning their lifestyle and provision for the future. Another influence is surely her faith and relationship with God and others. Still another is her own lifestyle. Are her values and lifestyle preferences realistic?

Susan's anger may or may not be sinful, but it is a feeling (an emotion or passion) that cannot be dismissed off hand. The *Catechism of the Catholic Church* teaches: "In themselves passions are neither good nor evil. They are morally qualified only to the extent that they effectively engage reason and will…. It belongs to the perfection of the moral or human good that the passions be governed by reason" (no. 1767).

At some point, Susan must realize that her anger presents her with a problem. With an informed conscience, she can determine (reason) that her anger, while a natural reaction, must be curbed and managed, even perhaps overcome. She has to decide (exercise her will) how she will handle the anger and the hurt which caused

Anatomy of a Moral Act

it. She can "stay mad" or she can put that anger to good use. For example, she may decide to help her parish reach out to families to help them provide better for their own futures. Also, she may be moved by grace to examine what she truly wants or expects out of life, what is truly a necessity and what is only enjoyable to have.

Besides anger, other principal *passions* are love and hatred, desire and fear, joy and sadness (cf. no. 1772). Depending on how we respond to those passions, they can result in good or in evil.

The "anatomy" of a moral or an immoral act is made up of three factors (cf. nos. 1750-1756). The three factors are separated here for the purpose of study, but in reality they occur simultaneously. First, there is the *object* to which one moves. Second, there is the purpose or the *intention* motivating the person. Third, there are the *circumstances* of the action, those elements which can increase or diminish the good or the evil of an act. Let's briefly examine each of these three factors, keeping in mind that St. Paul tells us to "do everything for the glory of God" (1 Cor 10:31).

The object chosen. What good does one want to obtain? What good is at stake for self or others? What personal pleasure or fulfillment is involved? We've all heard that the end does not justify the means. In other words, some acts are in themselves quite good, for example, giving Mom a gift on Mother's Day, or helping a fellow student pass a test. Those are good ends, but we can't steal to give Mom a gift and we can't let our friend copy test answers to pass a test. The end does not justify the means.

At the same time, we have to realize that certain objects (or ends) which we seek have moral value in themselves. They are either evil or good. For example, people have sexual passion. The desire for sexual pleasure is part of who we are, for God made us that way. Sexual pleasure, however, while good in a moral situation, is not by itself a total end. It is part of a greater good, the strengthening and celebration of love between husband and wife and the procreation of children. Adultery or fornication are immoral because they isolate sexual pleasure from the purpose and natural context of human sexuality. Fornication and adultery are evil in themselves. They are perverted acts whose goal is not to express love but to satisfy personal desire; they are sins in themselves and result from our human nature that was wounded and disordered by sin. As an expression of love between husband and wife, sexual intercourse, when open to life, is both fully human and holy. It expresses total self-giving love for the other. Couples have said again and again that physical pleasure in marital sexual love is heightened when sexual union expresses total, tender and compassionate love. Openness to life is evidence of great dignity in marital love, of deep faith on the part of husband and wife. Openness to life invites God into the relationship of love expressed in all daily activities which support and promote life, as well as in sexual union.

The intention motivating the person. In the above examples, the intention to give Mom a present and to help a friend pass a test are laudable and good intentions. However, in the case of adultery and fornication, the intention is evil because it seeks personal satisfaction regardless of moral considerations. An evil act can never be made good by good intentions. However, a good act can be made evil by evil intentions.

The circumstances involved in any action. The *Catechism* teaches that circumstances, which include the results or consequences of any action, are all part of the morality or immorality of that action. In other words, in adultery and fornication, the misuse of sexuality is as much a part of the action as is any physical pleasure. Theft committed to get Mom a present is a circumstance that renders the entire action immoral. Cheating to help a friend renders the entire act immoral.

Certain circumstances may lessen moral culpability, for example, pressure, duress, ignorance and fear. Other circumstances—such as more education, high public profile, greater economic solvency—may increase moral culpability.

For an act to be moral, three things must be present: its object (or goal) must be good and pleasing to God; the intention must be good and pleasing to God; the circumstances must not mitigate against goodness or limit the freedom of the person acting. The *Catechism* says that the circumstances can also diminish or increase the moral goodness or evil of human acts (cf. no. 1754). The amount of a theft and the financial condition of the victim affect the gravity of that sin. Stealing $100 from a wealthy person may not be as bad as stealing $10 from an unemployed father of a large family. Circumstances can also affect the degree of one's moral responsibility for an act. For example, it is always evil to take innocent life. However, one is also justified in defending one's own life against an unjust aggressor. In this second case, we are no longer talking about someone who is innocent but one who is assaulting with the intent to kill.

Reflection:

- When asked your opinion, how do you respond? "I feel..."? "I think..."?

- Why can relying only on feelings be inadequate in developing a strong moral life?

- Do people sometimes ignore feelings and cause pain?
- How would you advise someone who wants to balance feelings and objectivity?

Chapter 5

What Makes a Conscience Moral?

Tom was facing a major decision regarding a career change. His work with the State Department of Highways had security, but the pay was lower than he could get elsewhere. He and his wife, Judy, had four children, ages 10, 8, 5 and 2. Judy and Tom had decided she would not work outside the home until the children were older.

At the moment, they were paying their bills and were not under great pressure. The State had a retirement program and good health coverage. However, they wanted to live in a better neighborhood and put away more money for their children's college education. Their car was running, but it was old. They knew they would need a new car, but realized it would be hard to get one with their present income and obligations.

A major insurance company had offered Tom a job. The guaranteed salary was much larger than what he was making with the State and the commissions would have put him on easy street—if he were successful. He would have to work many more hours each week. He would get home late many evenings and would often have to travel. Of course, if he were not successful, the company would surely fire him.

Tom and Judy cannot see into the future, but they have to make a decision. What would be the right thing to do?

Every important life decision has a moral dimension. It is regrettable when people limit morality to decisions dealing with sex, killing and stealing. Tom and Judy face a moral dilemma in their decision about changing jobs. Much more than economics is involved. Marital stability, family strength and parental presence are all part of the picture. Tom may well make a morally sound decision in taking the insurance job. But he and Judy will have to plan their lives carefully to be sure Tom isn't away from home too often and miss the important events in the lives of their children.

If their consciences were properly formed, they could make a moral decision. It may not be the decision you or I would make, but it would be right for them, because they would do only what they knew they could do well and what was best for the family.

A moral conscience is essential for peace of mind. We have in our hearts and minds an innate sense of right and wrong. The Catholic Church teaches that moral conscience is necessary to live a good and wholesome life. A correctly formed conscience helps us know right from wrong and thereby directs us to proper choices. A moral conscience embraces God's will and commandments because it sees them as good. If one's conscience is properly formed, it sees God's commandments as beacons directing one to the greatest of all goods, of all beatitudes, God himself. A properly formed conscience rejoices in all that brings good to people and in all that brings people to God.

In Romans (2:13) we read: "For it is not the hearers of the law who are righteous in God's sight, but the doers of the law who will be justified." The Letter of James makes it clear that mere knowledge of God and lip service are of no avail:

> You believe that God is one; you do well. Even the

> demons believe—and shudder. Do you want to be shown...that faith apart from works is barren? Was not our ancestor Abraham justified by works when he offered his son Isaac on the altar? You see that faith was active along with his works, and faith was brought to completion by the works.... You see that a person is justified by works and not by faith alone (Jas 2:19-24).

Perhaps this quote from James points to the difference between simply an "informed" conscience and a "formed" conscience. It is not enough to *know* something is right or wrong; a Christian must *choose* and *act* upon what is right.

Conscience is not simply something within ourselves. A natural part of our very being, conscience is created in us and enlightened by God. In the words of Cardinal John Henry Newman, conscience is like a primitive vicar of Christ, a deeply imbedded sense of what is right and good, a tendency toward what is good. However, sin has upset the balance of nature and our conscience now must constantly renew its commitment to God and his will.

The *Catechism of the Catholic Church* reminds us that St. Augustine advised: "Return to your conscience, question it.... Turn inward, brethren, and in everything you do, see God as your witness." Once informed, conscience recognizes what is good by using human reason. The truth about what is good is not merely abstract but can be applied in concrete situations—past and present (cf. nos. 1779-1780).

But how does one form a good conscience? This is an important question. Some contemporary voices confuse formation of conscience with informing conscience, and freedom of conscience with no formation of conscience. To *inform* one's conscience, a Christian pursues knowledge of God. God's commandments and the Gospel of Jesus Christ become the central focus for informing conscience. God made us and loves us, so we know his will is what is best for us. In seeking God's will, we come to realize through the study of natural law that there is objective truth. The teachings of the Church help us learn and discern God's will in all things. We want an informed conscience so we can know which things are good and which are evil.

To *form* one's conscience, we have to discipline ourselves toward obedience out of love for God. We have to trust that God never wills anything that can move us away from him or test us beyond endurance. Formation of conscience is learning to live what we believe. It is learning to "live the good life," the life of grace, peace and harmony in and with God and one another.

As with anything worth attaining, a properly formed conscience takes effort, perhaps a little trial and error, loads of humility and constant self-discipline. We have to opt for a virtuous life, a life in which a person habitually seeks to do good and to avoid evil. Virtues enable persons to perform good acts and "dispose all the powers of the human being for communion with divine love" (no. 1804). Virtues will be discussed in more detail later.

The formation of conscience is a lifelong task. The *Catechism* teaches:

> Prudent education teaches virtue; it prevents or cures fear, selfishness and pride, resentment arising from guilt, and feelings of complacency, born of human weakness and faults. The education of the conscience guarantees freedom and engenders peace of heart (no. 1784).

Tom and Judy are faced with a moral choice—to remain with the State or take the job with the insurance company. We all face important moral decisions every day and have to make moral choices. How do we do that?

We can make "right judgments" based on reason and the divine law, or we can make bad judgments. Sometimes, as the *Catechism* says, circumstances can make a moral judgment less assured and a decision more difficult. But Christians always seek what is good and try to discern God's will expressed in divine law. Tom and Judy—and you and I—can be more assured of "right judgment" if we look at the reality of the situation objectively, pray for prudence (good judgment), ask the advice of competent people, and seek the Holy Spirit and his gifts.

Finally, when all this is done, the decision which offers the most peace of mind is usually the right decision. Further, the *Catechism* offers these rules which apply in every case: (1) never do evil for the sake of some good end; (2) as you wish to be treated, treat others; (3) respect your neighbor and never cause him to struggle or to stumble in matters of conscience, for to sin against a neighbor is to sin against Christ (cf. no. 1789).

Reflection:

- What examples in society indicate misinformed or uninformed conscience?
- Do you believe that one's conscience can be either properly or improperly formed? Please discuss with a friend.

Chapter 6

What Are Virtues? How Do We Become Virtuous?

The old priest looked thoughtfully into the eyes of the young man facing him, who was seeking spiritual direction. He had said, "Father, no matter how hard I try, I keep sinning. I keep making the same mistakes and falling flat on my face."

After a while, the priest said with a warm smile, "My young friend, when you fall flat on your face, you may still be pointed in the right direction."

Damaged by sin, it isn't easy for a person to maintain balance in life, to avoid sin once and for all. We are weak. We fail and fall. But the *Catechism of the Catholic Church* tells us that by seeking Christ's grace, frequenting the sacraments and surrendering to the power of the Holy Spirit, a person can learn to live a virtuous life (cf. nos. 1810-1811).

We may have a sense of right and wrong and be inclined toward goodness, but we are not automatically good. Consistently good (or virtuous) behavior is only developed through conscious effort.

To succeed better in living a holy life, we have to desire and seek the truth about good and evil. The ultimate truth is found only in God and in God's will, his divine plan for us. If we find and know the truth, we must make the right decisions about what we do or refuse to do.

And then, it is only by God's grace that we can hope to be good and holy.

God gives us three significant and indispensable "aids" or virtues that help us live good lives. These three virtues are the highest of all virtues, the foundation of all other virtues (or good qualities) in our lives. They are called the "theological virtues"—*faith, hope* and *charity*. These virtues enable us to believe that the old priest was right—that in desiring to know, love and serve God, even when we fail, we are "still pointed in the right direction." Faith, hope and charity pick us up from momentary failure and set our faces toward God once again with renewed determination and a healthier sense of dependence on God.

Faith, hope and charity (love) are gifts from God. Without God's free gift, we could never have faith (truly know God and believe in him), cling to hope (in eternal life) or experience love (the power that transforms us). These virtues prepare us to participate in God's own divine life and nature. Faith, hope and charity shape us to live in relationship with the most Holy Trinity. Our Triune God is the source, object and motive of faith, hope and charity (cf. no. 1812).

Faith (cf. nos. 1814-1816). We could never believe in God (as opposed simply to knowing God exists) without the gift of faith. Through faith, we come to know, love and serve God. We believe all that he has revealed and all the authentic teachings of the Catholic Church founded by Jesus, who is both the Son of God and the Son of Man.

However, faith without works is dead, as we read in the Letter of James (2:26). Without hope and love, "faith does not fully unite the believer to Christ and does not make him a living member of his Body" (no. 1815). As Christians, it is not enough to believe in God intellectually. Faith must become a part of life. We profess our faith openly and witness our faith to others.

Hope (cf. nos. 1817-1821). Each of us desires happiness. Hope responds to that natural desire. It is more than the sentiment expressed in everyday statements such as, "I sure hope it doesn't rain on my golf game." The virtue of hope enables us to desire eternal life in heaven and to believe we can attain eternal life through God's love and mercy. As we know, God is ultimate beatitude. In the Sermon on the Mount, Jesus gives us several beatitudes which help us hope for the everlasting kingdom of God. The beatitudes enable us to hope for spiritual growth and holiness here and now, in other words, to have something of the kingdom in our everyday life. Hope points us toward God and enables us to trust God.

Hope also gives us greater expectations from relationships forged in the love of God. In the Letter to Titus (3:6-7), we learn that God, through Christ, poured out upon us the Holy Spirit "so that, having been justified by his grace, we might become heirs according to the hope of eternal life."

Charity (Love; cf. nos. 1822-29*).* This virtue enables us to love God above all things and to love our neighbors as ourselves. God deserves all our love, and we love our neighbors because God loves them. Because we love God, we love whom he loves. Jesus said: "I give you a new commandment, that you love one another. Just as I have loved you, you also should love one another" (Jn 13:34).

Because Jesus loved us enough to die for us, and because he is the perfect revelation of the Father, we know that God the Father loves us. Jesus told us that he loves us as the Father has loved him (Jn 15:9, 12). Also, Jesus died for us while we were in sin—enemies of God. Likewise, we are to love our enemies (nos. 1822-1826).

Charity gives life and dimension to all the virtues, binding them together. Love gives form and direction to the other virtues. It cannot be limited only to God or only to neighbor. True love embraces God and neighbor. Love animates and gives life: "God is love, and those who abide in love abide in God, and God abides in them" and "those who love God must love their brothers and sisters also" (cf. 1 Jn 4:16, 21).

Charity liberates: The one who loves "no longer stands before God as a slave, in servile fear, or as a mercenary looking for wages, but as a son responding to the love of him who "first loved us..." (no. 1828).

Finally, God adds a finishing touch. He gives us the Spirit whose gifts are "permanent dispositions" that make us docile before God and cooperative with the Spirit's promptings. The Spirit's seven gifts are wisdom, understanding, counsel, fortitude, knowledge, piety and fear of the Lord. Jesus the Christ possesses these gifts in their fullness; we possess them to the degree we are obedient to God and open to the power of the Spirit (cf. nos. 1830-1832).

Reflection:

- "Charity liberates." Can you remember a time when someone's loving act freed you of guilt or fear? If you feel comfortable in doing so, share this experience with another person.

- How does hope differ from wishful thinking? What is hope rooted in?

CHAPTER 7

Natural Goodness and Grace

Robert had always been successful. He was a star athlete in both high school and college. When he entered the business world, he rose quickly into top management. He still persisted in rigorous physical exercise and he never tired of improving his mind. He had great discipline and was admired by all his associates.

During his college years, he and Mary, his childhood sweetheart, realized their relationship had forged a deep love. They began to think about marriage.

Two weeks after they graduated from college, Robert and Mary married. Their lifestyle and personal values evidenced serious thought and moral convictions: Mass on all Sundays and holy days; time for personal and family prayer every day; natural family planning to space their children; their decision that Mary would begin her nursing career when the children were older; a systematic savings plan no matter how small the income; tithing; assistance and support for neighbors and friends.

Were Robert and Mary virtuous?

Yes, this man and woman were virtuous. They seemed to have a natural inclination toward good. Their values showed respect for their own health and welfare. They showed signs of personal discipline and an openness to one another in making decisions.

They exemplify what we might call human or natural virtues that are rooted in a person's makeup, good behavior and values. These good virtues that seem to "come naturally," however, can become holy behavior only with God's help. When nourished by faith, hope and charity, the "natural" virtues are strengthened and bring peace and wisdom to human life. There are four "natural" or human virtues: prudence, justice, fortitude and temperance.

Prudence. Robert and Mary decided that she would stay at home with the children. This decision was difficult to make. Since it costs a lot of money to live and to educate children, two salaries would have meant a lot to the family. However, in their case, Mary and Robert decided that their children needed a sense of security. Mary's presence all day would give them that sense and also strengthen the family ties. They looked at all the facts and choose the greater good in their situation. That was the *prudent* thing to do. They were prudent because they sought the highest good through faith and trust in God. Also, they hoped for greater goodness later in life and in eternity—and their love for God and one another enabled them to see clearly what was best for their children and what would give them greater peace of mind now and later.

Prudence strengthens the intellect to discern between good and evil and to choose good over evil. St. Thomas Aquinas said prudence is "right reason in action." Prudence helps a person understand the boundaries between right and wrong and to discern the value or danger of certain decisions or actions. In this way, prudence supports all the other virtues. A truly prudent person is prudent habitually—or as a rule. Decisions are made thoughtfully and prayerfully as a matter of course.

If a person is not prudent, he or she can pray for prudence and expect to grow in that virtue with God's help. An imprudent person can grow by seeking advice from a trusted and prudent friend or advisor. Through prayer, the friend's guidance, and constant effort, a person can develop the virtue of prudence.

Prudence, the *Catechism* further states, "immediately guides the judgment of conscience." In other words, this virtue helps us apply moral principles in any given situation. That discernment can be free from doubt about the right and wrong of any situation when a person exercises faithfully the virtue of prudence. "The prudent man determines and directs his conduct in accordance with this judgment" (no. 1806). However, being human, a Christian realizes that consultation with others is often advisable so that discernment can be strengthened and even purified of personal prejudice and error.

Justice. A just person gives God and others their "due." In other words, God and others, even all of creation, are "due" certain things from us. God is due total faith, respect, love, trust and worship. He alone is God and we should not have false gods before him. Later, when we discuss the Ten Commandments, we will look more closely at what we owe God.

In the case of other people, we *owe* them respect, the right to life, and protection of their own human rights as we want ours protected. We owe them love because we are all creatures of the same loving Father who created us to belong to one another and to him. As the *Catechism* states:

> Justice toward men disposes one to respect the rights of each and to establish in human relationships the harmony that promotes equity with regard to persons and to the common good. The just man, often mentioned in the Sacred Scriptures, is distinguished by habitual right thinking and the uprightness of his conduct toward his neighbor (no. 1807).

We can readily see that for the Christian, a virtuous life is possible only through living as God would have us live. In speaking of the virtue of justice, the *Catechism* reminds us of Jesus' words: "Just as you did it to one of the least of these who are members of my family, you did it to me" (Mt 25:40).

The *Dictionary of Biblical Theology,* edited by Xavier Leon Dufour, sees justice as extending from the individual to the common good as well as from society to the individual. In other words, individuals must act in harmony with and out of concern for the common good, for the sake of others; society must act in respect and support for the good of each and every individual. The *Catechism* holds to that principle as well.

Fortitude. It is easy to see fortitude in the lives and deaths of the saints, particularly of the martyrs. However, the Holy Spirit gives us fortitude every day in all kinds of situations. Fortitude can help us overcome fear, even the fear of death. Fortitude also helps us to persevere in good works, to overcome temptation, and even to sacrifice one's own life for the sake of others. In the Gospel Jesus tells us, "In the world you face persecution. But take courage; I have conquered the world!" (Jn 16:33).

Robert and Mary must surely have experienced second thoughts and even hard times when they decided to live on one salary. Perhaps they had difficulty in remaining faithful to their decision to space children by natural and moral means—but their ultimate perseverance is due to God's grace. God gives them and us the fortitude (strength) to do what is right regardless of the cost.

Catholics who find it hard to talk about their faith with others may need a good dose of fortitude. The Holy Spirit can help us overcome timidity or a feeling of inadequacy. Like all the virtues and all of human goodness, fortitude is rooted in the very mind and heart of God. Love God, obey God, trust God—and the impossible becomes possible.

Temperance. Food, drink, ego and sexual appetites can and often do become obsessive in the modern world. Cajuns have a standing joke: "Most people eat to live; we live to eat!" While said in jest and with more than a little pride in our native cuisine, we Cajuns may well be speaking more truth than fantasy. Perhaps other ethnic groups may live to eat as much as Cajuns do!

Temperance is that virtue which enables us to use the good things in life—food, drink and sexual pleasure—as they were intended to be used: to support life and not to rule one's life. The *Catechism* teaches:

> The temperate person directs the sensitive appetites toward what is good and maintains a healthy discretion: "Do not follow your inclination and strength, walking according to the desires of your heart" (Sir 5:2; cf. 37:27-31) (no. 1809).

Do not follow base desires but master those appetites in a manner befitting a being of intellect and soul, as well as of body.

Finally, let's say it again. Human virtues are learned by education and the experience of trying consistently to do what is right. By perseverance, our efforts are purified and elevated above the natural by divine grace. "With God's help," our efforts, prayers and actions, "forge character and give facility in the practice of good" (no. 1810).

Reflection:

- Have you ever met anyone who seemed "naturally good"? Describe that person's values and behavior.

- When a person is touched by faith, what may happen to "natural goodness"?
- Did this chapter help you think more deeply about justice? If so, why?

Chapter 8

The Truth about Sin

A saucy octogenarian named Lucy was speaking with one of her daughters. Lucy had not been to church in twenty-three years. Her daughter, Susan, was trying to convince her mother she should come back to the Church. "Things have really changed, Mama. It's not like it was just after the Council when everything seemed up for grabs."

"Look," retorted Lucy. "It isn't the same Catholic Church anymore. When that new priest told us we couldn't say our rosaries at Mass, I knew it was no longer the same Church. Besides, I haven't killed anybody and I've never stolen anything in my life. I say my rosary every day. I think I'm okay with God and if not, then I don't know what more I can do about that. If God doesn't like me, then I can't change that. So, what's the use."

Susan had heard all this before. She didn't know what to do or say.

We've all heard or said ourselves what Lucy said. Sometimes, when we can't quite live up to what the Church or others ask of us, we become defensive. We stand on our own merits. We remind God and everybody about what is wrong with them and what is right about us.

In a word, that is self-righteousness. In another word, it is denial of sin.

St. Paul reminds us:

> But with me it is a very small thing that I should be judged by you or by any human court. I do not even judge myself. I am not aware of anything against myself, but I am not thereby acquitted. It is the Lord who judges me. Therefore do not pronounce judgment before the time, before the Lord comes, who will bring to light the things now hidden in darkness and will disclose the purposes of the heart. Then each one will receive commendation from God (1 Cor 4:3-5).

Concerned for her mother, Susan seems to avoid judging her mother. She seems to express genuine concern as she urges her mother to give God and the Church another chance. Lucy, for her part, has judged the Church and herself, and maybe even God.

If we judge ourselves, we probably will either condemn or excuse ourselves. God does not want to condemn: "God did not send the Son into the world to condemn the world, but in order that the world might be saved through him" (Jn 3:17). God does not *excuse* as we understand excusing. He does not deny what is good or evil. God understands both the motive of our hearts and our actions. He *forgives* us for doing what is wrong, even what is very evil—and that is marvelous and a cause for wonder. Such is God's merciful love. When God forgives, it is not just a light or half-hearted "Oh, you're excused!" No, it is this: "What you did, my child, was wrong. But I forgive you. I wipe it away. It no longer counts. I put your sin as far away from you as the east is from the west" (cf. Ps 103:12).

The *Catechism of the Catholic Church* defines sin as an act or thought which goes against reason and truth. It goes

The Truth about Sin

against a good, informed and formed conscience. Sin is failure to persist in love of God and neighbor. Sin damages our very being and divides us from one another (cf. no. 1849). In the Book of Genesis (3:5) we see that the first sin involved the desire of man and woman to be like gods. What is truly a sin is a choice of self over God; sin reflects one's sense of independence from God and denies God's lordship over his creatures (no. 1850).

The horror and violence of sin is uniquely manifested in its many forms in the betrayal, condemnation and death of Jesus:

> ...in the Passion...sin most clearly manifests its violence and its many forms: unbelief, murderous hatred, shunning and mockery by the leaders and the people, Pilate's cowardice and the cruelty of the soldiers, Judas' betrayal—so bitter to Jesus, Peter's denial and the disciples' flight. However, at the very hour of darkness, the hour of the prince of this world, the sacrifice of Christ secretly becomes the source from which the forgiveness of our sins will pour forth inexhaustibly (no. 1851).

One difficulty Christians face is life in a world that is insensitive to the reality of sin. The world is insensitive to sin because it does not take God seriously, no longer believes in the existence of the devil and places personal desire, whim and pleasure at the heart of one's existence. As a result of this calloused social conscience, far too many people accept all kinds of perversions as normal and of little or no moral consequence.

St. Paul gives us such a list:

> Now the works of the flesh are obvious: fornication, impurity, licentiousness, idolatry, sorcery, enmities, strife, jealousy, anger, quarrels, dissensions,

factions, envy, drunkenness, carousing, and things like these. I am warning you, as I warned you before: those who do such things will not inherit the kingdom of God (Gal 5:19-21).

Sin is real. It has eternal consequences. Some sins are so serious they are called mortal sins. Others are not so serious and are called venial sins.

> *Mortal sin* destroys charity in the heart of man by a grave violation of God's law; it turns man away from God, who is his ultimate end and his beatitude, by preferring an inferior good to him.
>
> *Venial sin* allows charity to subsist, even though it offends and wounds it (no. 1855).

A mortal sin is committed when the offense involves "a grave matter and...is also committed with full knowledge and deliberate consent." The Ten Commandments give us what is considered grave matter. As Jesus told the rich young man, it is sinful to commit adultery, steal, murder, defraud another or dishonor one's parents (cf. Mk 10:19). However, even if a sinful act is committed, unintentional ignorance may at times remove personal guilt and responsibility for sin.

> But no one is deemed to be ignorant of the principles of the moral law, which are written in the conscience of every man. The promptings of feelings and passions can also diminish the voluntary and free character of the offense, as can external pressures or pathological disorders. Sin committed through malice, by deliberate choice of evil, is the gravest (no. 1860).

It is sobering to realize that human freedom, which we so cherish, permits us to commit mortal sin, to turn our backs on God, the source, beginning and end of our own life. Love is also a "radical possibility" of human freedom. Since the fall of Adam and Eve, we have continued to struggle between sin and holiness, between inordinate love of self and unselfish love rooted in God's love.

Venial sin weakens charity even though charity can subsist with such sin. Venial sin is surely a less serious matter than mortal sin, but it harms us and limits our ability to grow and practice virtue. As the soul weakens and the conscience is compromised through "deliberate and unrepented" venial sin, a Christian becomes more susceptible to graver sin. However, venial sin does not deprive us of sanctifying grace. As such, through prayer and human effort we can receive forgiveness, repent and make reparation for such sin. Contrary to mortal sin, venial sins do not have to be confessed to a priest. On the other hand, Catholics who want to grow in holiness often do confess venial as well as mortal sin.

Finally, sin makes us more prone to sin (cf. nos. 1865-1869). Just as a small leak in a levee gradually becomes larger until the levee breaks and floodwaters pour in, so too, Christians who take small sins lightly soon find themselves assaulted by temptations and the growing possibility of grave sin.

The "capital sins" are so-called because they lead us into other sins. They are *pride, envy, greed, lust, gluttony, anger* and *sloth*.

Sin is always personal. Only we can commit our own sins. However, we are responsible for another's sin if we cooperate or encourage his or her sin. We are responsible for another's sin when we order them to do something wrong, or voluntarily participate in the sin, by not protecting the other person from sin or by protecting evil-doers.

Reflection:

- Do you believe in the reality of sin? If so, what are the major moral concerns in society today?
- Which areas of human behavior most urgently need the grace of repentance and amendment?
- If you were to write a "letter to the world," how would you help people recognize the reality of sin, the presence of God and the ability to change one's way of life?

Chapter 9

The Truth about Mercy

A long time ago, a wayward man finally had to face justice. He was charged with theft, convicted and condemned to death. Dismas trembled as he faced death. He knew he was a sinner and had wronged many people.

On the day of his execution he met Jesus, who was also condemned to death. Though innocent, Jesus had to die a criminal's death. A third man, another criminal, was also crucified the same day. That third man taunted Jesus. Even in his agony on the cross, he hated goodness enough to blaspheme the Son of God.

Dismas, however, told his fellow criminal that Jesus did not deserve those taunts, much less this shameful and torturous death. He begged Jesus for mercy.

Jesus immediately responded: "Today you will be with me in paradise" (cf. Lk 23:39ff.)

This beautiful gospel story echoes the words the angel spoke to Joseph when he learned that his beloved Mary was pregnant: "You are to name him Jesus, for he will save his people from their sins" (Mt 1:21). Again, Jesus himself spoke of his merciful love and sacrifice when, at the Last Supper, he took the cup of wine into his hands and said: "This is my blood of the covenant, which is poured out for many for the forgiveness of sins" (Mt 26:28).

We also have the passage so often quoted in calling people to surrender to God's love: "For God so loved the world that he gave his only Son, so that everyone who believes in him may not perish but may have eternal life. Indeed, God did not send the Son into the world to condemn the world, but in order that the world might be saved through him" (John 3:16-17).

Love expresses itself in mercy. The *Catechism of the Catholic Church* states clearly that mercy is a fruit of love (cf. no. 1829). However, Christians cannot presume on God's mercy. Christ made it clear that we totally depend on God for life here and hereafter. Also, Christ taught us that if we want to be forgiven, we must forgive others. That's explicit in the Lord's Prayer: "...forgive us our trespasses as we forgive those who trespass against us."

Since mercy is the fruit of love, a person without mercy is a person who fails in love. If one fails in love, he weakens his communion with God and others and weakens his ability to accept God's love and mercy. The Lord himself again reminds us that the way we treat others is the way we shall be treated ourselves (cf. Mt 7:2, Mk 4:24).

The *Catechism* reminds us that this communion of love is realized and strengthened through the power of the Holy Spirit (cf. no. 1109). At Mass when the priest calls upon the Holy Spirit to sanctify the gifts (which include all believers), we are called upon to believe in what is taking place on the altar: the bread and wine become the Body and Blood of Jesus Christ. But more! We are called upon to live this Eucharistic mystery in daily life. We bear the fruits of love (charity) in daily life. The fruits of charity are joy, peace and *mercy* (cf. no. 1829).

In a sense, mercy and love are almost synonymous. You cannot have love without mercy. Like love, mercy is a way of life. St. Paul said that love is the greatest virtue.

"Love is patient; love is kind; love is not envious or boastful or arrogant or rude. It does not insist on its own way; it is not irritable or resentful; it does not rejoice in wrongdoing, but rejoices in the truth" (1 Cor 13:4-6).

As we look at morality, it becomes increasingly clear that sin has a social dimension. Sin is not something that offends only God. Sin offends God in part because it hurts our neighbor. Sexual sin, too, hurts others. What is called love in cinema and art so often is only lust and selfishness. Yet we cannot limit the term "moral" only to sexual concerns. Any sin is immoral and goes against nature as created by God. It is immoral to hurt others, to deny people a just wage, to cheat an employer, to abuse a spouse or a child.

The *Catechism* gives a lot of space to "the human community," the relationship of a person to society, the common good and social life. The Holy Father and our bishops frequently address social, political and economic concerns. These are moral issues no less than abortion and sexual behavior.

Reflection:

- Reflect privately on how you may have ever felt like Dismas—guilty and condemned, and then suddenly forgiven.
- How does one's sin and righteousness affect family and society? Do you think people are aware of their connection with their community and all humanity?

Chapter 10

Morality and Society

"Big brother is watching you!" stormed the old farmer to his friends, pounding his fist on the table. He was angry because he felt he was "just another number" at the local bank. When he applied for a small loan for seed to plant his crops, he could not get it without giving the banker his social security number.

"I've been doing business with this bank for forty years," he had told the vice president in charge of loans. "I've always paid my debts on time. My name, a handshake and my signature was all that was needed. Now you want my social security number. You want to mortgage my land. That land's been in my family for more than 100 years. If you need more than a handshake and signature, you don't need my business!"

Our society and government have grown so complex that it's easy to "feel like a number," especially at income tax time. Our population has grown steadily. People live longer and need more assistance in old age. More children are born into poverty, and society often needs to help care for them. Communities wrestle with these problems that have no easy answers.

At the heart of it all, however, society must have as its primary concern the welfare of each individual. None of us is "just a number." If I am poor, I am not just one of millions of poor people. I am a human being feeling the pangs of poverty: hunger, poor health, frustration, despair, loneliness, powerlessness.

The *Catechism of the Catholic Church* teaches that each person needs to live in society (cf. nos. 1878-1880). We are social beings by nature. Made in the image of God who is Trinity, we are never completely happy or secure apart from others. We need each other. As Teilhard de Chardin wrote in *The Divine Milieu,* one person's need is another person's fulfillment. Each of us has natural gifts and talents that are given and exercised for meeting the needs of others.

As a society we are bound together by a "principle of unity" that goes beyond each one. A society lives in time, remembering the past, learning in the present and planning for the future. Part of a society's strength is that people with similar gifts, roles and concerns gather into smaller "societies" for their own welfare. But these smaller societies can also benefit the common good. Our fundamental "small society" is the family. Other small societies are the local neighborhood and the secular city. There are the state and geographic regions in which people share com-mon resources, needs and even dangers. There are professional and occupational societies in which people communicate and assist one another—medical associations, farm bureaus, bar associations. There are religious societies such as the Catholic Church, the Southern Baptist Convention and the Lutheran Missouri Synod. This gathering of individuals in sub-societies is called socialization.

All these sub-societies call individuals together for mutual support and should benefit all of society. The larger society is enriched or impoverished by individuals and sub-societies. Socialization can present dangers:

Excessive intervention by the state can threaten personal freedom and initiative.... [The] Church has elaborated the principle of *subsidiarity,* according to which "a community of a higher order should not interfere in the internal life of a community of a lower order, depriving the latter of its functions, but rather should support it in case of need and help to co-ordinate its activity with the activities of the rest of society, always with a view to the common good" (no. 1883, quoting *Quadragesimo Anno).*

Since God has decided to honor human freedom and let people do what they can for themselves, always giving them his gracious and divine assistance, so should government relate to sub-societies and individuals. Government should enhance the responsible exercise of freedom. People in authority should see in all individuals that special quality of human life which mirrors God. Leaders should see themselves as ministers of God's own divine providence. Anyone in authority must help people to help themselves and to exercise their right to self determination with the common good of all as a constant in governmental and individual efforts (no. 1884).

Back in school days, we all learned that "the whole is equal to the sum of its parts." Folk wisdom has it that "one bad apple can spoil a barrel." For society to be just and moral, the majority of its individuals must be just and moral. Even the greatest saints sinned and needed to repent. Every society has enough difficulty, injustice and immorality to occasion repentance and renewal. Society, like its members, needs conversion.

In his historic encyclical *Pacem in Terris,* Pope John XXIII said that human society was primarily concerned with the spiritual. Through society, "in the bright light of truth," people can fulfill their obligations, exercise their rights and be inspired to seek spiritual values. Society must make it possible for people to pass on their heritage and share their spiritual and material goods as well as their personal talents and gifts. Such order gives "aim and scope to all that has bearing on cultural expressions" such as political organizations, economic institutions and policies, the sub-societies already mentioned and "all other structures by which society is outwardly established and constantly developed."

Society and its members cannot confuse the "ends" and the "means" and people must never be used simply as means to an end (cf. nos. 1887-1888). To keep society strong for the sake of justice and the common good, it is essential that people strive for constant inner conversion. Through the conversion of individuals and their influence for the common good, worthy social customs and laws can be attained. Although personal conversion is of highest priority, social institutions are not excused from making any necessary changes in structure and actions which could compromise in any way the individual's ability to live a good, moral life.

As the *Catechism* states:

> Without the help of grace, men would not know how "to discern the often narrow path between the cowardice which gives in to evil, and the violence which under the illusion of fighting evil only makes it worse" *(Centesimus Annus,* 25).... Charity is the greatest social commandment. It respects others and their rights. It requires the practice of justice, and it alone makes us capable of it (no. 1889).

Modern people and societies need conversion. With God's help, may we embrace what is good, do God's will and bring sanity and sanctity to everyday life!

Reflection:

- Name some ways in which people can become "just another number" in today's society. What can be done to counteract this human isolation?
- Take a look at the modern world. Discuss ways in which groups, society as a whole or even nations have (a) shown cowardice or (b) reacted violently under the guise of combatting evil.
- Is a violent response to evil ever justifiable? Explain.

CHAPTER 11

Authority and the Common Good

A group of reporters and editors of Catholic publications had invited an archbishop to speak to them. One editor said that religious news centered around two concerns, the news about the *institution* and news about *real people living in the real world.* The archbishop quickly responded: "The institution is not lifeless. It is people committed to the common good. The institution of government is made up of people, of laws, of cultures; the institution of the Church is made up of people, of laws, of tradition and culture."

"It is not fair," the archbishop continued, "nor is it accurate to treat the institution as though it were lifeless, archaic and of no consequence. The institution is important to the survival of the society and, in our case, of the Church."

After Vatican Council II, it became popular to criticize the "institutional Church," namely the Pope and the college of bishops. Misreading the precise teachings and thrust of that great council, some people began to think the Church had suddenly become a democracy and that external or organizational renewal counted most.

On the contrary, when Pope John XXIII opened that symbolic window to let fresh air into the Church, he envisioned a spiritual renewal that would in turn give life and form to any changes that the council inspired in the Church's organization. Collegiality and liturgical renewal needed to build on the foundation of spiritual renewal.

Institutions and their leaders hold authority in society precisely to protect it and move it forward, to help people achieve their full potential and to promote and protect the common good. The *Catechism of the Catholic Church* clearly states that (1) each human community needs authority for its own governance; authority is rooted in human nature and is necessary for unity and for the good of all, or, the common good; (2) "the authority required by the moral order derives from God" and people must obey authority that is rooted in the moral order; and (3) people are to respect those in authority as they exercise their power of governance in a moral way (cf. nos. 1898-1900).

Moreover, the *Catechism* teaches that the type of government and who will lead the governed are the choices of the citizens themselves (cf. no. 1901). Legitimate authority is not self-made. It comes first from God and second from the governed. Vatican Council II taught that authority must act as a "moral force based on freedom and a sense of responsibility." St. Thomas Aquinas wrote that a law that "falls short of right reason" is not only an unjust law but lacks the nature of a law and, what's more, is more like an act of violence (cf. no. 1902).

Citizens sometimes feel insecure when their major political parties seem more concerned about power struggles than the common good. Different political parties can be good for society as long as they are all working for the common good and exercising authority in a moral manner.

What do we mean when we speak of the "common

good"? Is the common good more important than the welfare of the individual? The *Catechism* holds that when we speak of the common good we are speaking also of the good of each individual (cf. no. 1905). The good of the individual can be understood properly only in terms of who a person is as a child of God, as a human being who possesses certain inalienable rights.

The common good consists of "three essential elements," according to the *Catechism* (cf. nos. 1907-1909):

• There must be *respect for the person*. Public authorities must respect the "fundamental and inalienable rights" of each individual regardless of race, color or creed. Each member of society must be free to pursue his or her vocation in life. Each person must be able to exercise those "natural freedoms" such as the right to follow one's conscience and the right to practice religion freely.

• *Social well-being* and *development of the group or society* are all part of the common good. While promoting the good of each individual and group, legitimate authority must settle differences. While doing this, society must be sure that everyone has what is needed for life: food, clothing, shelter, health, education, employment, adequate information and the right to establish a family, to name some of the most obvious rights.

• *Peace* is a requirement of the common good. Peace, for the common good, comes from a moral and just order which provides "stability and security." Authority must insure the security of society and its members by just and moral means. That need for security is the basis "of the right to legitimate personal and collective defense."

Finally, society must be concerned about persons before it is concerned about any system of order or governance. Human beings are the focus and reason for government and authority. Therefore, social justice is a legitimate concern. Some Catholics are upset when the Pope and bishops comment on seemingly "political or economic" concerns. However, all human life and concerns have moral consequence and the Church rightfully addresses these concerns. Jesus was quick to recognize injustice; the Church must also recognize injustice and promote social justice.

The questions of war and peace, of economic conditions and policies, of the right to life are all of moral consequence. As the *Catechism* holds:

> Respect for the human person entails respect for the rights that flow from his dignity as a creature. These rights are prior to society and must be recognized by it. They are the basis of the moral legitimacy of every authority: by flouting them, or refusing to recognize them in its positive legislation, a society undermines its own moral legitimacy. If it does not respect them, authority can rely only on force or violence to obtain obedience from its subjects. It is the Church's role to remind men of good will of these rights and to distinguish them from unwarranted or false claims (no. 1930).

The fundamental principle fueling social justice is that each person must look upon others as "another self." Each person is neighbor to all others. It's captured in the old pledge of the Three Musketeers: "All for one and one for all." As the parable of the Good Samaritan asks, "Who was neighbor to the victim of the assault?" *Neighbor* is a proactive role, not merely one of receiving from others. The Good Samaritan was the good neighbor because he went out of his way to help "another self" who was a stranger and an alien (cf. Lk 10:29ff.).

The *Catechism* takes up this theme when it states:

> The duty of making oneself a neighbor to others...
> becomes even more urgent when it involves the
> disadvantaged, in whatever area this may be. "As
> you did it to one of the least of these my brethren,
> you did it to me" (Mt 25:40; no. 1932).

A community that calls itself Christian has no room for discrimination against people because of racial, ethnic, sexual, educational or economic differences. Vatican Council II's document *Gaudium et Spes* states that all forms of social or cultural discrimination in recognizing human rights "must be curbed and eradicated as incompatible with God's design" (no. 1935).

The virtue of charity is ignored and set aside when people discriminate against one another. The cross of Jesus Christ seals this law of charity and the basic solidarity of all humans who come from the same Creator and are called to the same destiny (cf. no. 1939).

It becomes increasingly clear that the "institution of the Church" is vital to Christians and to society as a whole. The Church reminds us of our common origin, our common nature and the common destiny to which God calls us.

The archbishop quoted in the story above was on solid ground. The institution is crucial to survival for the individual and for all society. Each person in society and in the Church has a responsibility to participate in the life of society and the ecclesial community, to serve the common good according to one's opportunities and gifts (cf. nos. 1913-1917).

Reflection:

- Are there signs of racism in your home, school or community?

- What other injustices exist, if any?
- Discuss with your spouse or a friend your understanding of "institution" and its value to life. Has your understanding changed over the years?

Chapter 12

The Moral Law: What Is It?

"Tell the Pope to get out of my bedroom!" shouted the angry woman who challenged a speaker on natural family planning.

- "It's my body!" exclaimed a woman confronting a sidewalk counselor in front of an abortion clinic. "I have a right to choose what happens to my body!"
- "Just let the Pentagon send airplanes and wipe out all those Serbs! That will solve the problem!" argued a man who had never been to war.
- "Look, it's a bottom line question," said the up-and-coming young executive. "Just cut salaries by ten percent and lay off three percent of the work force. That will increase profits."
- "What's the difference?" the grocery clerk said. "So I take a few groceries home with me from the supermarket. I'm underpaid anyway. As far as I'm concerned, it isn't stealing, it's justice!"

What's wrong with those statements? It is true people have a right to privacy and no one wants a stranger in his or her bedroom. But a moral teaching is not the same as invasion of privacy. It's also true that a person's body is sacred and one has a right to nourish, clothe and protect one's body. However, a baby in the womb is not a woman's body and the divine command not to kill another person surely protects the innocent and defenseless baby in the womb.

Freedom-loving people throughout the world want an end to conflict, war and oppression. In the case of the Serbs fighting the Bosnians and Croatians, thousands of innocent people suffered. However, indiscriminate bombing is no solution to violence. Isn't violence a strange solution to violence? No wrong can be made right by another wrong.

Likewise, all employers have the option to cut employees' salaries and lay off workers. But are these moral and sensitive options? Don't people have the right to work? Isn't human dignity tied in with that right to work for a living wage? What obligations do employers have in dealing with their employees—and what is the basis for recognizing those obligations?

In the case of the grocery clerk, stealing is stealing, regardless of the reasons. If a family is starving, a father or mother may not be culpable of sin by taking food to feed the children. However, stealing from an unjust employer to compensate for low wages is hardly as extenuating a circumstance as starvation.

We all have to be moral in our relationships and concerns. Laws are made to order human relationships, to protect the rights and lives of individuals and to move a society forward. The "laws of man" find their foundation in the laws of God, in the moral law. "Moral law" comes from God and it is written in the heart of each person. It is not oppressive, as some would say. The *Catechism of the Catholic Church* calls it God's fatherly instruction and pedagogy (cf. nos. 1950-1953).

Divine and human law can help people achieve their full potential on earth and then communion with God for

The Moral Law: What Is It?

all eternity. Moral law is rooted in reason, in the very nature of who we are as creatures of God. We are repulsed by evil and violence and moved with pity for those who suffer. We embrace loved ones with a passionate desire to protect and nourish. We respect the rights and property of others because each person is "another self" to us, so to protect others is to protect ourselves.

There are different and interrelated expressions of the moral law. The eternal law derives from God and is the source of all law. Then there are natural law, revealed law (God's Word in the Old and New Testaments, or the Law of the Gospel), and civil law and Church law.

For Christians, the New Law or the Law of the Gospel fulfills the Old Law. It gives new meaning to the Ten Commandments which are the heart of the Old Law. In Christ, Christians find the way to perfection. Jesus himself said, "I am the way, and the truth, and the life" (Jn 14:6). He fulfills the law; he is the ultimate end of the law because he teaches and bestows the justice of God: "For Christ is the end of the law so that there may be righteousness for everyone who believes" (Rom 10:4).

Let's look briefly at the natural moral law. Later, we'll consider the Old Law, and the Law of the Gospel.

The Natural Moral Law (cf. nos. 1954-1960). God made us in his image, and God is not inactive. Made in his image, we are alive and can observe, think, reason, decide and act. God gives us mastery over our actions so that we might direct our lives according to what is right, true and good.

The natural law is "divine and natural" in that it comes from God and is placed in the heart of each person. The natural moral law stems from a desire for God and for full surrender to him. That quest for meaning in life and for peace of mind and heart is the impetus of the divine and natural law which urges us toward God who is our beginning and end.

That's why the Ten Commandments (which we will treat later) are so important to us. These commandments express the fundamental precepts of the natural moral law. The precepts of this law undergird our conscience and focus our spirit on truth. The natural moral law is not "natural" in the sense that it comes from humans; it is "natural" in the sense that it is part of human nature as created by God. The *Catechism* quotes Thomas Aquinas:

> The natural law is nothing other than the light of understanding placed in us by God; through it we know what we must do and what we must avoid. God has given this light or law at the creation (no. 1956).

The defensive statements made by people (such as those above) are in themselves admissions of error. Any conviction or action that requires self-centered defense is to be held suspect. When we speak of "my right" and "my body" when moral questions are raised, it is time to look at the rights of others and God's "rights" to our love and obedience.

Such defensiveness may be rooted in a guilty conscience, since even the most uninformed conscience recoils in the face of evil. Each person has a fundamental inclination toward the natural law in the human heart and soul. It is universal in its precepts and extends to all peoples at all times (nos. 1955-1956).

Reflection:

- Why is a moral teaching not an invasion of privacy?
- Can you give an example of how people demonstrate "natural law" in their relationships?

- Discuss how the Ten Commandments lay the foundation for expanded moral teaching. Do the Ten Commandments in any way relate to the Beatitudes?
- Define "the natural law." (See "The Natural Moral Law" in this chapter.)

CHAPTER 13

Old Law and Gospel Law

The grandson saw the old man's face redden with anger. "What do you mean," demanded the grandfather, "that love has replaced God's Ten Commandments?"

"Well," said the boy, "that's what our religion teacher said. She said that Jesus told us to love one another. That was his new commandment. We must love one another as he loved us and as he and the Father love one another."

"But that doesn't wipe out the commandments," said the grandfather, now regaining his "cool," as his grandson might say. "God's commandments were given to Moses and are meant for all time. This love business does not negate them!"

Isn't is wonderful when both people are right in an argument? No, not unless both people realize they are both right and begin to understand how both positions express the same truth. Here grandfather and grandson are both correct. The commandments were given for all people of all time; Christ did give us a "new commandment," that we love one another as he loves us.

The Old Law. The problem comes in with different understandings of law and love. The *Catechism of the Catholic Church* gives us a beautiful exposition of the Old Law and the Law of the Gospel or the law of love (cf. nos. 1961-1974).

God's will begins to be revealed to us in the Old Law. Its moral directions are codified briefly in the Ten Commandments, which give foundation to our lives as men and women fashioned in the image of God. They forbid what is contrary to God's will and his love for us as well as love of neighbor. The Law is good and holy. But as the *Catechism* says, it "does not of itself give the strength, the grace of the Spirit, to fulfill it. Because of sin, which it cannot remove, it remains a law of bondage." However, as St. Paul tells us (cf. Rom 7:12, 14, 16), the Law reveals to us what is sinful. The *Catechism* says that "the Law remains the first stage on the way to the kingdom. It prepares and disposes the chosen people and each Christian for conversion and faith in the Savior God. It provides a teaching which endures for ever, like the Word of God" (no. 1963).

The Law of the Gospel. Here is where the grandson in our story is "coming from." He has heard the Law of the Gospel and he believes it. His grandfather, on the other hand, realizes that "love" does not always mean the kind of love Christians experience and propagate. He is concerned that his grandson realize that "the Law of the Gospel is the perfection here on earth of the divine law, natural and revealed. It is the work of Christ and is expressed particularly in the Sermon on the Mount. It is also the work of the Holy Spirit and through him it becomes the interior law of charity" (no. 1965). This catechetical definition of the Law of the Gospel echoes what St. Augustine once said: "Love and do what you will." In other words, if we love as God loves, if we are completely submissive to God's will, we will do what God wants us to do. We will embrace the commandments by a new way of life, a life born of love in the heart redeemed by the blood of Christ, a life renewed and empowered by the very Spirit of God.

This new Law of the Gospel is grace, the grace of the Holy Spirit through faith in Christ. This law finds its energy and expression in Christ. Its motivating force is charity, or love.

The Sermon on the Mount, and especially the Beatitudes, are embraced in fidelity and love as the normal way in which Christians live. The divine promises given as results of living the Beatitudes (...the kingdom of God is theirs...) are fulfilled in the New Law because they are now clearly oriented to the kingdom of God. It is now clear why God gave us the Ten Commandments. The New Law makes the Old Law less burdensome and fearful. The old has been kissed by the new and a new life has been born.

The *Catechism* teaches this about the commandments:

> The Lord's Sermon on the Mount...releases their hidden potential and has new demands arise from them: it reveals their entire divine and human truth. It does not add new external precepts, but proceeds to reform the heart, the root of human acts, where man chooses between the pure and the impure, where faith, hope and charity are formed and with them the other virtues. The Gospel thus brings the Law to its fullness through imitation of the perfection of the heavenly Father, through forgiveness of enemies and prayer for persecutors, in emulation of the divine generosity (no. 1968).

The Sermon on the Mount, as well as the Ten Commandments, come down to us through the Church. It is fitting, indeed, when looking at "the Law," both Old and New, to include the teachings of the apostles and their successors throughout the history of the Church. What comes to us from God in Scripture and Tradition and the authentic teachings of the Pope and bishops is to be embraced as part of the Law of the Gospel (cf. no. 1971).

Finally, the Law of the Gospel is indeed a *law of love*. We act out our faith through love infused in us by the Holy Spirit as we enter into and express faith in our sacraments and other liturgies. It is also a *law of grace* because it gives us the strength and power to do what God asks us to do. It is a *law of freedom* because we act freely and spontaneously out of charity, rather than restriction and fear as was too often the case under the Old Law.

So, the grandfather and the grandson are both right, but they may both be wrong as well. If the grandfather has not embraced the liberating power of the Spirit in the Law of the Gospel, he has not yet adequately incorporated his own redemption and liberation. If the grandson has not embraced the Old Law as foundational and directional and a guide for living out the New Law, then he may well have missed the point Jesus made so clearly: "Do not think that I have come to abolish the law or the prophets; I have come not to abolish but to fulfill" (Mt 5:17).

Reflection:

- Does this chapter help you understand better how the Gospel liberates us from law, as St. Paul teaches? Explain.

- Do you see more clearly the relationship between the Ten Commandments and the Beatitudes?

Chapter 14

To Be Justified by Grace

At 2 A.M., the middle-aged Catholic clergyman rose from bed with a belligerent attitude. He had not been sleeping well, nor had he been praying well lately. For more than six months, prayer had been sporadic and perfunctory at best. "Well," he said to himself, "if I can't sleep anyway I might as well get morning prayer out of the way!"

He opened his breviary and the first line he read "jumped out" at him. "Surrender to God and he will do everything for you."

He spent the next thirty minutes reflecting on that one line: "Surrender to God and he will do everything for you."

After a while, the clergyman knew what his problem was. As an old preacher said, he had been working for God instead of trying to do God's work. He realized that while working for God, he could put himself first and do what he wanted to do and fool himself into thinking it was what God wanted him to do. But if he put God first and sought God's will, he might have to put his own personal agenda on the back burner.

Everything about our life is spiritual. The body and the spirit, the psyche and the soul are so closely linked that it is virtually impossible to do anything that is totally physical (or emotional) or totally spiritual. This fact is important for Christians who want to grow spiritually.

On the one hand, we find people who conveniently divide themselves into body and soul, flesh and spirit. With such division, a person can learn to hate the body and put the soul on such a high plane it somehow becomes something other than part of the whole person. On the other hand, some people forget that we are both matter and spirit and that the matter is sanctified by God as our souls and spirits are sanctified by God. We are totally human. That means body and soul are equally part and parcel of our humanity. That's why the body will be resurrected at the Last Judgment, because with only the soul or only the body there would be no human being, no person to be judged and given an eternal abode.

To grow in wholeness and holiness, we must realize that God does the sanctifying, the justifying and the saving. We do not save ourselves. We cannot earn God's grace. The clergyman in our story may well have been trying to make himself holy, to use his own gifts, exclusive of God's help, to accomplish the goals in his life.

What does it mean to be justified, to be sanctified? The *Catechism of the Catholic Church* has an easy to read and excellent treatment of grace and justification (cf. nos. 1987-2011). It is well worth reading carefully and prayerfully. What follows is a brief explanation of that section of the *Catechism*.

To be sanctified is to be made holy. To be justified is to be cleansed of all our sins. This is possible only through faith in Jesus Christ who, by his life, teaching, passion, death and resurrection, has redeemed us and made it possible for us to be reconciled to the Most Holy Trinity.

In the Holy Spirit we die to sin as we are immersed through baptism into the death and resurrection of Jesus.

With the power of the Holy Spirit, we participate in the divine nature. St. Paul said it so well: "For through the law I died to the law, so that I might live to God. I have been crucified with Christ; and it is no longer I who live, but it is Christ who lives in me. And the life I now live in the flesh I live by faith in the Son of God, who loved me and gave himself for me. I do not nullify the grace of God; for if justification comes through the law, then Christ died for nothing" (Gal 2:19-21).

To observe the commandments apart from faith in Jesus Christ does not justify a person. Only in accepting Jesus as Lord and Savior can a person be delivered from sin and made holy. Justification is a gift which we must seek, receive and protect. The truly frightening thing about freedom and free will is that we can refuse God and his salvation, and thus choose self and damnation.

The entire benefit of justification in the Blood of Jesus includes sanctification and renewal of the inner man as well as forgiveness of sins. "Justification detaches man from sin"; it requires that we accept God's righteousness; it has been merited for us by Jesus Christ in his passion, death and resurrection; justification "establishes cooperation between God's grace and man's freedom." It is the gracious work and gift of God "manifest in Christ Jesus and granted by the Holy Spirit" (no. 1990-1994).

It is said that Americans especially find it difficult to believe that grace, justification and salvation are free gifts of God. Our work ethic and "rugged individualism," as well as the contemporary self-centeredness, lead us to believe that we have to work for everything; we are also led to believe that we deserve whatever we desire. Yet we have "no strict right to any *merit*" from God, for there is "an immeasurable inequality" between us and God. What merit we have comes from God freely deciding to involve us in his work of grace. What merit we achieve stems first from God's gift to us and only secondarily from our decision to say "yes" to God. What love God has for us! (cf. nos. 2006-2011).

If people can encounter God's love through the Church, and that means all who believe, if they can begin to understand that life, grace and salvation are *gifts* from God—things they could never earn—they would begin to find peace.

Our clergyman in the story at the beginning of this chapter may have forgotten this important truth: Grace and salvation are pure gift; we do nothing to deserve them; we are invited and urged by a loving God to *accept* them for the sake of eternal happiness. We are justified by faith in Jesus Christ; we are sanctified by God as we live in his love and by loving as he loves. Sanctification comes from union with God and his will. Holiness requires that a person embrace God. Jesus said: "I am the way, and the truth, and the life" (Jn 14:6). We are not first of all Christian and holy by what we do, but by what we believe and how we respond in faith. While holiness is a gift, it is "gift-wrapped" in God himself. That gift can be "opened" only if we become "gift-wrapped" by God. In other words, we must know God, love God and serve God. We must do his will—and when we fail to be and do what God wants us to be and do, we must renew our justification. We must confess our sins, repent, make amends and move forward toward eternal life holding the hands of Jesus and our Mother, Mary.

Reflection:

- Discuss the definition of justification by faith.
    - a) Have you heard this term before? From whom?
    - b) Did the term mean much to you then?
    - c) What does "justification by faith" mean to you now?
- We want to be in union with God. What did the clergyman learn to do?

Chapter 15

The Church, Mother and Teacher

The catechist was instructing a group of young adults in the faith of the Church, using the Apostles' Creed as a text. During a discussion period on "life everlasting," someone raised a question about purgatory. The catechist briefly explained the Church's teachings on purgatory.

A woman in her early twenties said, "Well, I graduated from a Catholic high school and our theology teacher said there was no such thing as purgatory. He said that when you die you go to heaven or to hell and that's it."

If this young woman understood her theology teacher properly, he was not fulfilling his responsibility. Those who teach the Catholic faith must teach what the Church teaches, not what they or some dissenting theologians have to say about Church teaching. Catechesis is not about private opinion. We have the Church, our mother and our teacher, to guide us in our understanding of God and his revelation of himself to us in Scripture and Tradition.

Unfortunately, in recent years, authentic teachings of the Church have been treated only as "opinion" with no more weight than the opinions of theologians who may or may not agree with the teachings of the Church. A high school theology teacher is not a bishop in communion with the Holy Father and all other bishops, nor is a priest or lay theologian.

The first duty of any Catholic who seeks to preach and teach the truth is to be faithful to the teachings of the Magisterium of the Church. "Magisterium" means the teaching authority of the Church—the Holy Father and all the bishops in communion with him. The *Catechism of the Catholic Church* teaches:

> [The Magisterium] in moral matters is ordinarily exercised in catechesis and preaching, with the help of the works of theologians and spiritual authors. Thus from generation to generation...the "deposit" of Christian moral teaching has been handed on... (no. 2033).
>
> The Roman Pontiff and the bishops are "authentic teachers...endowed with the authority of Christ, who preach the faith to the people entrusted to them, the faith to be believed and put into practice." The *ordinary* and universal *Magisterium* of the Pope and the bishops in communion with him teach the faithful the truth to believe, the charity to practice, the beatitude to hope for (no. 2034).

When the Church teaches infallibly, the Magisterium is participating in the "supreme degree" of the authority of Christ. The Church's power to teach infallibly covers the extent of divine revelation. In other words, the Church has the power of Jesus, through the guidance of the Holy Spirit, to teach natural law as well as the content of true doctrine and the precepts of our faith. That's the responsibility of the Pope and the bishops. The rest of us—clergy and laity, theologians and catechists—have the duty of observing what is conveyed by the legitimate authority of the Church. "Personal conscience and reason should not be set in opposition to the moral law or the Magisterium of the Church" (cf. nos. 2035-2040).

The Church provides us with six rules or "precepts" which are "in the context of a moral life bound to and nourished by liturgical life" (no. 2041). As Catholics, we have an obligation to obey these precepts because they help us conform our lives to the will of God. Briefly, these precepts are as follows (cf. nos. 2042-2043):

1. *You shall attend Mass on Sunday and holy days of obligation.* By observing this precept, we show obedience to the commandment to keep holy the Sabbath Day. Also, we are joining our fellow Catholics in offering praise and petition to God. The liturgy is the high point of Catholic life because we experience our faith in community, foster and strengthen unity, and celebrate and strengthen love.

2. *You shall confess your sins at least once a year.* Older Catholics will remember being required to "make their Easter duty," which meant they went to confession and received Communion during Lent or the Easter season. Actually, a Catholic is required to go to confession only if he or she is in the state of mortal sin. Therefore, this precept is very lenient; it tells us the minimum we should do. Happily, today many Catholics receive Communion at least weekly. However, the number of Catholics who go to confession regularly is at an all-time low. The Sacrament of Reconciliation is a powerful way to meet Jesus, to receive forgiveness of sins and to experience reconciliation with oneself, God and the Church. It is common pastoral practice to recommend confession at least once a month—and, of course, Catholics must go to confession before receiving communion when they are guilty of mortal sin.

3. *You shall humbly receive your Creator in Holy Communion at least once a year during the Easter season.* This "Easter duty" was linked with mandatory confession in the minds of many Catholics, perhaps because if they hadn't been to

confession or received Communion in a whole year, they felt a need to confess before receiving Communion. The Eucharist is a great sacrament in which we receive Jesus Christ in his fullness—his humanity and divinity. The sacrament received worthily sanctifies and strengthens us in unity and charity.

4. *You shall keep holy the holy days of obligation.* The Church singles out holy days even though they are already covered in the first precept. But "holy days" cover much more than the "holy days of obligation" which require Mass attendance. There are feast days of various saints. Keeping those days holy may mean extra reflection in prayer on the life of that particular saint, doing an act of mercy or charity in imitation of the saint. Keeping any day holy means a day-long task, not just a thirty minute Mass or a ten-minute rosary.

5. *You shall observe the prescribed days of fast and abstinence.* Following this rule helps Catholics to practice restraint over appetites and self-control in preparation for the Church's feast days such as Christmas and Easter. This precept helps us strengthen mastery over self and to maintain true freedom, which lies only in obeying God's will.

6. *We also have the obligation to support financially the work of the Church's mission.* In recent years, stewardship has become more and more the way in which Catholics approach Church support. *Stewardship* teaches us that all we have—money, time and talent—are gifts from God given to us, his stewards, to use for our own needs, the good of others and the propagation of the faith. Church support, or stewardship, is a way of life more than a function, a task or an isolated obligation.

Finally, our faithfulness to the Gospel and all the teachings of the Church are essential to the mission of the Church. If we do not live what we believe, our preaching

The Church, Mother and Teacher

and witness will be lifeless and without authenticity. Our faithfulness and divinely inspired and empowered good works have the power to draw others to the faith. We build up the Church through our constant fidelity to truth. "By living with the mind of Christ, Christians hasten the coming of the reign of God" (nos. 2044-2046).

Our holy Catholic Church is indeed our mother and teacher. In the Church, we receive life through the sacraments and the Word of God and we are guided confidently and faithfully in Jesus Christ who is the Way, the Truth and the Life.

Reflection:

- How do we draw others into our holy faith?
- Do you believe the Church is both mother and teacher? Explain.
- Review privately the six precepts of the Church and how you, at present, respond to them.

CHAPTER 16

A Look at the Ten Commandments

All I have to do to get to heaven is to observe the Ten Commandments. I don't need the Church and CCD and anything else like that. That's all the result of the work of human beings. The Ten Commandments say it all!

That's how one man responded to an invitation to go to Mass after many years of absence. In a sense he was right. The Ten Commandments say it all—but not so clearly and so thoroughly that God was content to end revelation with Moses' visit with him on Mount Horeb. God continued to reveal himself throughout the Old Testament. His final revelation of himself was in Jesus Christ, in whom we have the fullest revelation of God. In Christ, we find the fulfillment of all the law and the prophets.

People who focus on the very limited and "negative" content of the Ten Commandments can miss the fullness of what God wants and intends for us. Jesus surely obeyed all the commandments. In fact, he expanded on them, especially in the example of his life and in his preaching. Note especially his Sermon on the Mount which contains those wonderful Beatitudes. We began *We Live the Good Life* with a reflection on the Beatitude who is God and on the Beatitudes which help us to be like God and to do God's will.

The *Catechism of the Catholic Church* places the Decalogue, (literally Ten Words, what we know as the Ten Commandments), the Sermon on the Mount and the apostolic catechesis together as "paths that lead to the Kingdom of heaven. Sustained by the grace of the Holy Spirit, we tread them, step by step, by everyday acts..." (no. 1724). We also read: "The Beatitudes confront us with decisive choices concerning earthly goods; they purify our hearts in order to teach us to love God above all things" (no. 1728).

Christians are obliged to obey the Ten Commandments. But the Church has learned over the years that each commandment is broader in scope than it appears at first glance. We have solid teaching from the Magisterium to show this. We will look more closely at each of the commandments and will try to understand better how the "Two Great Commandments" accurately capture the spirit of all Ten Commandments. A Pharisee tested Jesus by asking him which was the greatest commandment. Jesus replied:

"'You shall love the Lord your God with all your heart, and with all your soul, and with all your mind.' This is the greatest and first commandment. And a second is like it: 'You shall love your neighbor as yourself.' On these two commandments hang all the law and the prophets" (Mt 20:34-40).

As we examine the Ten Commandments, we will understand better why Jesus said that the law and the prophets depend on these two great commandments. The importance of the Ten Commandments is further emphasized by the fact that God chose to reveal them specifically while they were already known to the heart of man as part of the natural law (cf. nos. 2070-2071). Through reason we can determine that each of the Ten Commandments is true and good for humanity to follow. But God chose to give us the commandments through Moses because human reason and will are tainted and weakened by sin.

The Ten Commandments are not mere suggestions. They are "fundamentally immutable, and they oblige always and everywhere... The Ten Commandments are engraved by God in the human heart" (no. 2072).

An alcoholic in a drunken stupor once said: "It's God's fault I'm this way. He can't blame me for being a drunk. God made me!"

The story goes that this poor man finally joined Alcoholics Anonymous and turned his life over to God. In surrendering to God, he found victory over his disease and his need for alcohol.

The man at the beginning of this reflection said he didn't need the Church because he had the Ten Commandments. The drunk said his sin was God's fault. Both were victims of error, and they were kidding no one but themselves. God does not demand what we cannot do with his help. As the *Catechism* says, "What God commands he makes possible by his grace" (no. 2082).

Reflection:

- Do you know someone who has overcome a serious problem through prayer and grace? Reflect on that person's victory.

- Discuss the value of the challenges of the Beatitudes.

- The Beatitudes, Ten Commandments and the teaching of the apostles are "paths that lead to heaven." Why? How do they relate?

Chapter 17

Our Relationship with God

The old grandfather stood in the background, holding in his hand a weathered piece of wood cut into the shape of a boat. He had carved that little toy for himself when he was only nine years old. Years later, his own son had played with it. As his son grew older, the grandfather put the miniature boat away in a nook in the garage. "Someday," he had thought, "my grandchild will play with that boat."

With love he looked at his grandchild running along the ditch filled with recent rain water. The child was pulling a big, shiny plastic boat a neighbor had given him. It was a new toy, its smooth lines glinting in the sun. But sadness tinged the grandfather's face. The crude boat he held in his hand was not pretty and shiny, but it had been carved in wonder and enjoyed by two young boys. It had love in its rugged lines, memory, and, yes, fidelity. The grandchild had turned away from it when the neighbor had showed up with the shiny new plastic boat.

God is not an old man up in the sky. God is pure spirit. But he is our father and perhaps, in a way, even our grandfather. He loves us passionately and provides for us as a father does. He also loves us with a gentleness only a grandparent can know.

God wants us to know him and love him. As the old Baltimore *Catechism* taught us, "God made us to know him, to love him and to serve him in this life and to be happy with him forever in the next."

To know, love and serve God is to hold him in deep reverence, and to realize he has no beginning and no end. He is Creator, Redeemer and Comforter. The first of the Ten Commandments calls us, as God's creatures and children, to recognize him alone as God. The Commandment reads:

> I am the Lord your God, who brought you out of the land of Egypt, out of the house of slavery; you shall have no other gods before me. You shall not make for yourself an idol, whether in the form of anything that is in heaven above, or that is on the earth beneath, or that is in the water under the earth. You shall not bow down to them or worship them... (Ex 20:2-5).

Jesus reminded us of this great commandment when he confronted Satan: "Worship the Lord your God, and serve only him" (Mt 4:10).

The God who loved his people enough to liberate them from slavery in Egypt is the same God who loved us enough to send Jesus to redeem us. This loving God indeed loves fiercely and without condition. He desires only that we love him in return and worship him alone. This is not a selfish God. He calls us to surrender to him because only in him can we find fulfillment as human beings.

Although we know from the teachings of our Church that God is supremely happy, it doesn't take much imagination to understand how we can offend him by turning our backs on him, and the ancient truths and remedies he holds for us in his hands. The grandfather in our story felt sadness and maybe anxiety for the grandchild so easily swayed by passing glamour. Somehow, we can see God feeling sadness, in the midst of his supreme happiness, when we set aside his way, truth and life, to pursue some passing glitter and glamour.

We learn from the Church in this first commandment that when we acknowledge God and stand before him in awe, we are drawn into faith, hope and charity: *faith*, because to say "God" is to confess this supreme, unchanging, holy, loving, just and omnipotent being who reveals himself to us as a loving Father and deliverer; *hope*, because we depend on God to help us respond to his love with our own love; *charity*, because faith in God's love leads us to respond in love to God and all his children, indeed to all his creation (cf. nos. 2086-2093).

Sins against the first commandment

People sin against faith by nourishing doubt in God and revealed truth, by a certain cynical or prideful hesitation to believe ("Show me!") and the willful refusal to assent to the truth revealed by God and taught by his Church.

People sin against hope when they despair of God's mercy, thinking that they could commit a sin that not even God could forgive. (Carried to its extreme, despair may render a person incapable of receiving God's forgiveness because that person will not ask for it or be open to receiving it.) Also, presuming God's mercy can be a sin against hope. Presumptuous persons will fool themselves into thinking God will forgive them with no effort on their part to repent and reform. Presumption also leads people to believe they can save themselves.

We sin against charity when we refuse to acknowledge, prayerfully consider and be grateful for God's great love for us. We also sin against charity when we are lazy in returning God's love and in loving others. It is also sinful to be spiritually lazy or slothful and refuse to let our souls soar with joy in God's love. Finally, pride can lead us actually to hate God and all his love and goodness.

The *Catechism* is also very clear on the sinfulness of superstition, idolatry, divination and magic. For example, it is superstitious to believe that a rabbit's foot or a "devil's horn" can bring good luck or ward off evil spirits. Some people attribute divine power, which rests only in God, to these objects. It is also superstitious to believe that merely going through the external motions of prayer constitutes prayer and worship. True prayer requires proper spiritual dispositions.

Likewise, all forms of *divination* are against the first commandment. Scripture is clear about dabbling in anything that puts us or any other creature above God:

> No one shall be found among you who makes a son or daughter pass through fire, or who practices divination, or is a soothsayer, or an augur, or a sorcerer, or one who casts spells, or who consults ghosts or spirits, or who seeks oracles from the dead. For whoever does these things is abhorrent to the Lord; it is because of such abhorrent practices that the Lord your God is driving them out before you (Deut 18:10-12a).

For his own good purposes, God can reveal the future to saints and prophets, but the Christian must be willing, ready and able to place himself in the hands of Providence (cf. nos. 2110-2117) in the present moment and let God take care of yesterday and tomorrow. One of the beautiful things about the Lord's Prayer is that it places the past, present and future in God's hands: *past—*

forgive us our trespasses; *present*—give us this day our daily bread; *future*—lead us not into temptation.

How we obey the first commandment

The *Catechism* teaches: Faith, hope and charity "inform and give life to the moral virtues. Thus charity leads us to render to God what we as creatures owe him in all justice. The *virtue of religion* disposes us to have this attitude" (no. 2095).

We obey the first commandment by being truly religious as daughters and sons of God. We first of all *adore* God, who is supreme life, love and holiness. He is Creator, Redeemer and Healer, the Lord, the Master of all creation. To adore God is to be in absolute submission to him, to recognize his divinity and our dependence on him for existence.

Adoration must lead us into *prayer,* which is a way of adoring God. We cannot truly pray if we do not adore God. A Christian will offer different kinds of prayer at various times: praise and thanksgiving, intercession and petition (cf. no. 2098).

Also, we adore God through certain promises and vows. For example, the sacraments of Baptism, Confirmation, Matrimony and Holy Orders involve promises or vows. People sometimes don't realize that a man and woman, taking marriage vows and pledging fidelity and love for life, are making a promise to God and to each other and in making that promise, they are adoring God!

Reflection:

- Name some ways in which people may succumb to idolatry.

- Elvis, the "king," still has a large following. Can this be dangerous to one's faith? Why? Why not?
- Reflect on any "false gods" in your own life. What can you do to refocus your faith, hope and love?

CHAPTER 18

Our Relationship with God: The Second and Third Commandments

A young man once borrowed $5,000 from the local bank in a small rural community. The bank president knew the family. Because the young man's father was honorable, a man of his word, the bank did not require collateral. The father's name was enough for the banker. He trusted the son to be like the father.

Unfortunately, after several payments, the young man failed to honor the debt. The father was embarrassed; the banker was also embarrassed because he knew the father would honor his son's debt even though he was not legally bound to do so. The irresponsible son had sullied his father's good name.

Whether parent, grandparent or friend, many people have suffered at the hands of loved ones. Children and grandchildren, employees and employers sometimes fail to live up to ideals or commitments—and they cause pain and disappointment.

After God told us in the first commandment that he is the only God and we are to worship him alone, he gave us two more commandments governing our relationship to our loving and holy God. The second commandment is *"You shall not take the name of the Lord your God in vain."* The third commandment is *"Remember the Sabbath Day, to keep it holy....*" The first three commandments deal with our relationship with God. The following seven commandments govern our relationship with our neighbors.

In the second commandment, God tells us not to use his name in vain. He has treated us as intimate friends and family members because he has revealed his name to us. If you are among strangers whom you do not trust or whom you may never see again, it would be most unlikely that names would be exchanged. To give someone your name is to become both available and vulnerable to that person. That is why, for example, some people do not want their phone numbers published. They do not feel comfortable having their names available to anyone who comes along. The same element of trust is involved when prison ministry groups channel prisoners' pen pal letters through the ministry's mailing address. It is sometimes considered dangerous for the average person to give his address to a convicted felon.

Though we have time and again proven ourselves untrustworthy, our Father continues to give us his name so we can call on him, pray to him and experience intimacy with him. With this great trust from God, it becomes clear that abuse of God's name is a sign of ingratitude and irreverence, and it may even be blasphemous. We learn in the *Catechism of the Catholic Church* (cf. nos. 2142-2149) that we should respect God's name because it is the same as respecting the mystery of God himself. When he names himself as the Lord who will have mercy on whom he will, and as the Lord who delivered Israel from Egypt, he is speaking the reality of himself.

Christians witness their reverence to God's name by confessing their faith regardless of difficulties and dangers. Also, teaching the faith must include respect and adoration for the name of Jesus Christ the Lord.

We are not to abuse God's name, or the names of Mary or any of the other saints. Many modern movies, and people in daily life, often use the name of Jesus Christ as an expletive. What shabby treatment for the God-Man who died so that we might have eternal happiness! Or, people will often say, "By God" in any trivial matter and even in anger. When God's name is used as an oath (invoking God as witness to a promise, vow or event), it must be a serious matter and a holy concern, not a curse, a sin or a mere expression of exasperation.

Blasphemy is a serious offense against the second commandment. As the *Catechism* teaches, blasphemy "consists in uttering against God—inwardly or outwardly— words of hatred, reproach, or defiance; in speaking ill of God; in failing in respect toward him in one's speech; in misusing God's name" (no. 2148). It is also blasphemous to speak against Christ's Church, the saints and sacred things and to use God's name to cover up crime or lies, to oppress people or to torture or execute people.

When we are baptized, we are given a name for all eternity (cf. nos. 2156-2159). That name, given when we were baptized *"in the name of the Father and of the Son and of the Holy Spirit,"* is like a claim ticket God holds for each one of us. To call us by name is to acknowledge we are God's and God is our Father. We should use our own name and the names of other people in a respectful, loving and even reverential way.

The third commandment tells us to keep holy the Sabbath Day. "The seventh day is a sabbath of solemn rest, holy to the Lord" (Ex 31:15). It is holy to the Lord in this way: The Lord commanded Israel to keep the Sabbath in memory of their deliverance from Egypt; it was to be a day of rest for all, even animals (God seems to be against "workaholism"). For Israel, the Sabbath was a sign of God's irrevocable covenant to be their God and to care for them; it was to be a day in which people stopped to reflect on God's love for them, his presence and power in their lives.

For us Christians, Sunday, as a day of rest, is one way of reminding ourselves that everything we have comes from God. It shows our willingness to be like God—he rested on the seventh day and we rest on the Sabbath. We show trust in God when we observe Sunday as a holy day and a day of rest. We don't have to work ourselves to death to make a living—God provides and helps those who help themselves. (God even helps those who cannot or will not help themselves!)

We observe Sunday rather than the Sabbath because Jesus rose from the dead on Sunday. Sunday is the Lord's Day, the first day of all days (cf. nos. 2174-2176). By observing Sunday with worship at Mass and spending quiet time with family and friends, we give "an outward, visible, public and regular worship" to God who gives to all his goodness and gifts. Sunday is so holy that it is called the "foremost holy day of obligation in the universal Church" (no. 2177).

Sunday is observed primarily by participation in the sacrifice and celebration of the Mass. Jesus rose from the dead on Sunday, it is fitting that we celebrate his passion, death and resurrection on that holy day. This is so crucial to our lives as Catholics that the Church obliges attendance at Mass. Sunday worship should be done with an open, generous and willing heart. However, a limp spirit on any given Sunday is no excuse to stay away from Mass and the power of God present in the worshipping community. In fact, a limp spirit is all the more incentive for rushing to Church on Sunday!

Reflection:

- What would happen if stores were open on Sunday, but nobody came? Do you shop on Sundays? Is it really necessary? What does unnecessary Sunday business do to family life—yours and the clerks in the stores?

- Have you ever written a letter to the local newspaper critical of the abuse of God's name? Why? Why not?

- Name two things you could do to show and promote reverence of God's name.

Chapter 19

Our Relationship with Our Neighbors

A farmer had two sons. He asked the first one, "Son, would you please go out to the barn and clean out the stalls? The hay and manure are too deep and the filth is not good for the horses." The son responded, "Of course, Dad, right away!" But the son went into the hay loft and took a nap.

The father, thinking the first son was hard at work, asked his second son, "Son, would you kindly go muck out the pig sty and hen house? It's so bad in the pig pen that even the hogs are holding their breath, and in the hen house, the chickens don't want to come down from the roost!" The son responded angrily, "I most certainly will not! I'm no hired hand! Get the help to do it!"

But after a while, the second son realized how shabbily he had treated his father, so he changed his mind, got a shovel and cleaned out the pig pen and the hen house (cf. Mt 21:28ff.).

Lack of respect for older people is a major problem in contemporary society. In the past, young people respected their elders. They quickly stood when an adult entered the room and would never address an adult by his or her first name. Children knew better than to take the best chair for themselves when an adult was in the room.

Maybe it was a little one-sided in favor of adults, but the code of etiquette helped children remember they still had a long way to go and a lot left to learn. It helped children realize that adults were their ticket to life, health, education and wisdom.

In the fourth commandment, God tells us: "Honor your father and your mother." The *Catechism of the Catholic Church* says that this commandment "shows us the order of charity. God has willed that, after him, we should honor our parents to whom we owe life and who have handed on to us the knowledge of God. We are obliged to honor and respect all those whom God, for our good, has vested with his authority" (no. 2197).

A few years ago, Pauline Books & Media graciously published *Do Whatever He Tells You,* a book I wrote which, in part, reflected on the Ten Commandments. While writing about this commandment, it came to me that we must honor our parents also because they are our link in creation. Through them, we are connected to Adam and Eve, to Abraham, Isaac, Jacob and to the human nature of Jesus himself. When our parents bring us to the Church for baptism and worship, they bring us to our spiritual mother through whom we receive the sacraments, the Word of God and membership in the Mystical Body of Christ.

This fourth commandment is the first of those which deal with our relationship with other people. It is, in a sense, the springboard into right relationships. If the primal social relationship between parents and children in the family is made holy and healthy, then people will find it easier to honor and respect others. The commandment is expressly related to the relationship between parents and children because this is the most universal relationship.

"It likewise concerns the ties of kinship between members of the extended family. It requires honor, affection, and gratitude toward elders and ancestors. Finally, it extends to the duties of pupils to teachers, employees to employers, subordinates to leaders, citizens to their country, and to those who administer or govern it" (no. 2199).

If children respect parents and if parents love and protect their children, society has a strong foundation upon which to grow. If the home breaks down, and this commandment is not observed, then society suffers "great harm to communities and to individuals" (no. 2200).

A good marriage produces a good family, which is the basic unit of society. In the Church, we call the family a "church in miniature" and a reflection of the community and communion of the Most Holy Trinity, Father, Son and Holy Spirit (cf. no. 2205). As a basic unit of society and of the Church, the family must participate in the life of society and the life of the Church. In the family the marriage of Christian moral principles and involvement with secular society is best accomplished.

The *Catechism* teaches:

> Authority, stability, and a life of relationships within the family constitute the foundations for freedom, security, and fraternity within society. The family is the community in which, from childhood, one can learn moral values, begin to honor God, and make good use of freedom. Family life is an initiation into life in society (no. 2207).

In an age in which the number of older people is increasing dramatically, it is important for grown children to care for their aged parents and grandparents. As much as possible, grown children must give material, moral and spiritual support to their aging parents, especially when they are sick and lonely.

In the Bible we read: "For the Lord honors a father in honor above his children; and he confirms a mother's right over her children. Those who honor their father atone for sins; and those who respect their mother are like those who lay up treasure. Those who honor their father will have joy in their own children, and when they pray they will be heard. Those who respect their father will have long life; and those who honor their mother obey the Lord" (Sir 3:2-6).

At the same time, parents are responsible not only for bringing their children into the world but also for their health, education, security and Christian formation. Parents must see their children as children of God. By being good Christians who love and obey God, they teach their children a right relationship with God and with one another. Parents are the first evangelizers of their children. They hold first responsibility for the education of their children, which begins in a home filled with love and faith. It extends to the parents' involvement with schools and with the secular community and local, state and national governments.

I recall a touching scene I once witnessed in a hospital. The man and his wife were in their mid-thirties. They had married later in life than most do. Now they were in a maternity ward and a nurse was bringing in their first baby, a little girl. The nurse handed the infant to the new mother as the proud father leaned over his wife and child. Tears streaked the faces of both parents. The father put his lips close to his infant daughter's ear and whispered, "Jesus." He straightened up and said, "That's the first word I wanted her to hear from my mouth, the name of Jesus."

That makes the point, does it not?

The *Catechism* is a great source for a more thorough treatment of the relationships of parents, children and society (nos. 2196-2257).

Reflection:

- What conditions in your community or family weaken the relationship between parents and children?
- As the first evangelizers of their children, how can parents help bring them closer to the Lord?
- The family is regarded as the basic cell of the community and society as a whole. What can families do to strengthen society?

CHAPTER 20

You Shall Not Kill

In Sanford, just north of Orlando, a mother had to make a choice with serious moral dimensions. She discovered she had breast cancer the same day she found out she was pregnant with her fourth child. She refused surgery and chemotherapy until she was sure her unborn child would live.

The child did survive, but she did not. Her four children are now being raised by a trusted relative. Christians and other people of good will offered assistance to the family.

What a moving story! What a contrast to what society approves today—that women and their doctors kill unborn children in their mothers' wombs. What a contrast to the entertainment media which portray selfishness and violence as sophisticated and acceptable social behavior.

Jesus once said there is no greater love than to give one's life for the sake of another (cf. Jn 15:13). This woman demonstrated that great love, and we are richer for her generosity.

The Florida mother could have decided, and without violating moral principle, to receive treatment even though it endangered her unborn baby. Her decision to receive treatment would have been directed at preserving her own life. It would not have been a direct attack on the life of the baby. Any harm done to the baby, even its death, would have been an indirect consequence of the treatment. This is not the case in abortion when the object of the procedure is to kill the innocent baby in its mother's womb. Abortion is the direct taking of innocent life. It is immoral, and a crime against humanity, regardless of the motivation.

The *Catechism of the Catholic Church* clearly states that "since the first century the Church has affirmed the moral evil of every procured abortion. This teaching has not changed and remains unchangeable." The *Catechism* gleans from early Christian teachings: "You shall not kill the embryo by abortion and shall not cause the newborn to perish" (no. 2271).

The fifth commandment states, "You shall not kill." Some people try to apply this commandment only to the murder of innocent people. Some, on the other hand, see this commandment in opposition to any killing, even in a just war. Some others even believe they should themselves die at the hands of a murderer rather than kill in self-defense. A few others believe it is improper even to kill animals for food.

What precisely does the Catholic Church teach about the fifth commandment?

First of all, human life in itself is sacred from its very beginning. As the *Catechism of the Catholic Church* teaches, God is the author of life and is the only one who can decide when a person's earthly life is to end. No one has the right to take innocent life. However, a person can defend himself against death at another's hand, even if it means killing the aggressor. The intent is to preserve one's life, not to take the life of another (nos. 2258-2265). That principle also extends to entire societies (no. 2266) because "the common good of society requires rendering the aggressor unable to inflict harm."

So, while the Church is against killing, it recognizes that individuals and even entire nations have the right to defend their life, even if it means striking a lethal blow against the unjust aggressor. In no instance, however, is it ever justified or moral, even in war, to take the life of innocent people.

In contemporary times, the Church has expanded its emphasis on the sacredness of all human life. The "seamless garment" philosophy, introduced into American discussion by the late Cardinal Joseph Bernadin of Chicago, holds that even the life of a murderer and terrorist is sacred. In the last few decades, the Church's Magisterium has spoken out against the death penalty for capital crimes, holding that all human life is sacred. Pope John Paul II affirmed this in his encyclical *The Gospel of Life*. It is the life of a criminal that is sacred, not how he has perverted this great gift from God. Jesus himself said that he did not come to condemn people but to save them (cf. Jn 3:17). We frequently admit that we are to hate the sin but love the sinner. How can we love the sinner and still kill him?

Since human life is sacred and we are made in the image of God, why do people sin against this commandment? Original sin disrupted that divinely established order in human nature, an order in which the powers of mind and body were properly subordinated to right reason. Due to original sin, human nature was weakened and made prone to sin. Thus it was that Cain fell victim to pride and envy and killed his brother. Since the Fall and that first murder, the world has experienced all sorts of evil.

The right to life extends to all persons in all circumstances. It extends to masses of people as well. Hence we all have an obligation to see that the needs of the hungry, the sick and the homeless are met. This is an international responsibility of the human family. No one person, no nation should be denied the necessities of life. Hunger, famine and pestilence lead to death, war, and all sorts of violence. These conditions are a sin against human life. Anyone who is able to alleviate such injustice and human suffering but does nothing is guilty of a sin against human life.

The *Catechism* states:

> The acceptance by human society of murderous famines, without efforts to remedy them, is a scandalous injustice and a grave offense. Those whose usurious and avaricious dealings lead to the hunger and death of their brethren in the human family indirectly commit homicide, which is imputable to them (no. 2269).

Our Catholic faith also teaches us that euthanasia is morally wrong. Only God has the right to end a human life. "Whatever its motives and means, direct euthanasia consists in putting an end to the lives of handicapped, sick, or dying persons. It is morally unacceptable" (no. 2277). Of course, our faith makes a distinction between direct taking of life and merely disconnecting extraordinary life support systems when there is no hope for the patient to live on his or her own, no matter how long these medical procedures would be sustained.

As part of our response to the fifth commandment which forbids us to take human life, we are also obliged to take care of our own health and to avoid life-endangering habits such as smoking, excessive drinking, and illegal and unhealthy use of drugs. And, as Christians, we are obliged to practice safety on the highways, at work, and in the home and school.

For a thorough treatment of the fifth commandment, please see the *Catechism of the Catholic Church,* numbers 2258-2329.

Reflection:

- Consider your everyday relationships at home, school and work. In what way does violence manifest itself—even subtly?
- Do you think there is such a thing as a just war? Which wars fought in your lifetime were just? Which were not?
- Do you agree that selfish people and nations are responsible for the sufferings of less fortunate people? Why or why not?
- What in your opinion captured the interest of so many millions of people in the O. J. Simpson trial?

CHAPTER 21

Sexual Fidelity: In Spirit and in Deed

The young man had wanted to be a doctor as long as he could remember. He had finished medical school while his young wife had slaved hard to help him achieve his goal. Now he was interning in a major hospital, but he was being ridiculed by his peers. Everyone, true to soap opera form, seemed to be sleeping around. Married men and married women were breaking their vows repeatedly without chagrin. Because he was faithful to his wife, they thought he was strange, square, a wimp or a nerd.

This young doctor was a man of principle. He took seriously his vows and his responsibility. He loved, appreciated and revered his wife. He could not do anything to hurt her. In fact, if his principles ran true to Christian form, he viewed any infidelity on his part as a violation of his own person.

The *Catechism of the Catholic Church* speaks of the "integrity of the person":

"The chaste person maintains the integrity of the powers of life and love placed in him. This integrity ensures the unity of the person; it is opposed to any behavior that would impair it. It tolerates neither a double life nor duplicity in speech" (no. 2338).

Sin hurts the sinner. When a Christian sins, he or she may well feel self-betrayed. When a person goes against a good conscience and acts immorally, it is a betrayal of who and what that person really is and wants to be.

Remaining sexually pure in today's society is perhaps more difficult than in past generations—more difficult but far from impossible. One of the greatest enemies of sexual purity is the general social conviction that people can do anything they want to do as long as "it doesn't hurt anybody else." Supporting that erroneous conviction is the belief that there are no moral certainties, that the person is the sole authority on what is right and wrong for himself or herself.

Today's society has a juvenile fascination with sex, among people of all ages. Cinema and television productions focus on sex as the be-all and end-all in human relationships. (Goodness! Even Superman is now sexually involved!) Any fidelity in sitcoms or films is based mostly on humanistic values. There is a terrible lack of any serious and respectful attention to Judeo-Christian moral principles. If God is taken to exist, he is portrayed as either a tyrant bent on making people suffer or a puppet to satisfy their every whim. People with little or no religious education and weak family ties may be easily swayed by the media's distortion of human sexuality and morality.

God is clear about sexual morality and about the relationship between men and women. The sixth commandment states boldly, "You shall not commit adultery." It seems helpful to tie in another commandment with this particular discussion. The ninth commandment, reduced to its primary emphasis as learned from the old *Baltimore Catechism*, tells us: "You shall not covet your neighbor's wife."

There are no if's, and's or but's. Adultery is a sin. It is not acceptable in any society, much less in one which claims to have Judeo-Christian roots. Likewise, lusting after another man's wife, or another woman's husband, is sinful. It is akin to adultery. Whoever lusts after another has already committed adultery in his heart (cf. Mt 5:27-28). Experience shows that even "flirting" can lead to marital discord, regardless of whether or not actual physical infidelity ever occurs.

God created the human race, both male and female. Each is part of what it means to be human. The *Catechism* teaches:

> Each of the two sexes is an image of the power and tenderness of God, with equal dignity though in a different way. The *union of man and woman* in marriage is a way of imitating in the flesh the Creator's generosity and fecundity.... All human generations proceed from this union (no. 2335).

In holy Matrimony, a husband and wife sacramentally respond to God's call to "be fruitful and multiply" (Gen 1:28). The fruitfulness of their marriage is realized in two primary ways: in the procreation of children and in a growing bond of love between man and woman, which itself influences both the home and society.

As Christians, we are to be sexually pure, or chaste. For single people, that means abstinence from sexual relations; for married people, it means total fidelity one to the other and an openness to procreation of new life.

If a person is not true to himself, he cannot be a good witness of fidelity to God (cf. no. 2346). True charity, that is, love of God and others, as well as a healthy love of oneself, is the foundation and source of all the other virtues and of all loving acts. Chastity gives room for friendships to grow, precisely because it is born of love and respect for self and others. Perhaps especially in marriage, chastity helps husband and wife be true friends rather than mere sexual partners, cohabitants of the same house, and parents of the same children.

The *Catechism* lists the following sins against chastity: lust, masturbation, fornication, pornography, prostitution and rape. The Church further states that homosexual persons are called to chastity (cf. nos. 2351-2359).

Sexual intercourse is moral and legitimate only when it is performed by husband and wife in love and openness to God's will as far as new life is concerned. The *Catechism* teaches:

> Called to give life, spouses share in the creative power and fatherhood of God. "Married couples should regard it as their proper mission to transmit human life and to educate their children; they should realize that they are thereby *cooperating with* the love of *God the Creator* and are, in a certain sense, its interpreters. They will fulfill this duty with a sense of human and Christian responsibility" (no. 2367).

Our faith further states that when it is necessary to regulate births, not for selfish reasons but for serious ones, only natural means of spacing children may be used. Artificial contraception is an offense against the integrity of those who employ it and an offense against God. For example, use of chemicals, diaphragms or condoms is strictly forbidden.

The marriage act is as truly spiritual as it is physical (cf. nos. 2360-2363). It expresses the innermost being of husband and wife and their loving union. "In marriage the physical intimacy of the spouses becomes a sign and pledge of spiritual communion. Marriage bonds between baptized persons are sanctified by the sacrament." This is the real meaning and nature of sexual love.

Sexual Fidelity: in Spirit and in Deed

What passes for love in society is often not love but lust, not giving but taking, not natural but perverted, not a result of freedom but a sign of enslavement to base instincts and to sin itself.

Besides adultery, the *Catechism* lists the following offenses against marriage: divorce, polygamy, incest, so-called trial marriages, and free unions in which man and woman refuse to give judicial and public form to their union.

Reflection:

- What, if anything, is wrong with the term "making love"?

- Have you taken time to reflect carefully on the Church's teachings on human sexuality and marital love? If not, do you think it would be a good idea to do so?

- Can you see how love might be at times better expressed by abstinence rather than sexual relations?

CHAPTER 22

Don't Even Want What Your Neighbor Has!

A young man had listened carefully to his father's complaints about being poor. The father had convinced himself that rich people had money because they were corrupt. He accused them all of being crooked and of abusing their employees.

The young man adopted his father's attitude. He almost hated rich people and coveted their money and power. He hated his own way of life, his own financial limitations. He believed that anyone with money was crooked.

One day, he met a rather wealthy man who enjoyed his money, but also enjoyed giving it away. The rich man shared his goods with others and would even lend ordinary people his expensive automobile. The young man and the rich man became friends. Through this friendship, the young man finally realized he was the selfish one, since he did not share his own possessions. He was both envious and greedy—he wanted what others had and desired more and more.

He finally realized his poor father had been wrong. The young man found peace when he finally realized how wealthy he was: he was loved; he loved; he had precious personal gifts and skills; he had the opportunity to share what he had and to enrich his own life by enriching the lives of others.

The seventh, ninth and tenth commandments are specific about our relationships with our neighbors and their possessions. While these commandments overlap a bit in Scripture, the *Baltimore Catechism* listed them as follows:
- You shall not steal.
- You shall not covet your neighbor's wife.
- You shall not covet your neighbor's goods.

The *Catechism of the Catholic Church* provides prophetic teaching for our own times. Capturing the traditional teachings of the Church in a succinct and clear manner, the *Catechism* reminds us today how easy it is to violate the commandments against stealing and coveting what belongs to others:

> Even if it does not contradict the provisions of civil law, any form of unjustly taking and keeping the property of others is against the seventh commandment: thus, deliberate retention of goods lent or of objects lost; business fraud; paying unjust wages; forcing up prices by taking advantage of the ignorance or hardship of another (no. 2409).

To protect oneself against the temptation to steal or to covet, our faith tells us that we are to practice the virtues of temperance and justice. By our nature as social beings, we are created to live in solidarity with one another. Individual welfare and the common good demand that we respect the rights and property of others. The welfare of individuals is everyone's legitimate concern—thus, the obligation to pay just wages, to respect people enough not to take advantage of them. The common good is everyone's concern: we must sacrifice occasionally for the sake of others.

Justice is so much more than what is demanded by law. It is more than the often and erroneously quoted Old Testament notion of "an eye for an eye and a tooth for a tooth." Justice means to give everyone his or her due. Each individual has a right to life, to liberty, to food and shelter, to education, to freedom of worship and assembly. In justice, we must see that each person's rights are honored and his or her needs met. Justice demands that society, all of us together, give each person his due. That's why the Church supports government programs that try to meet the massive needs of the poor at home and abroad.

Pope Paul VI once said that the wealthy are using goods that rightfully belong to the poor. This does not contradict Church teaching that we all have a right to private property. This papal statement is rooted in the kind of justice that comes from charity, temperance and solidarity. As the *Catechism* states (no. 2403), the right to private property "does not do away with the original gift of the earth to the whole of mankind."

We break the seventh commandment, then, by directly taking or keeping what belongs to others, and indirectly by paying unjust wages, hoarding public resources, denying the rights of any individual or any ethnic group, and even by unwarranted military or political takeover of weaker nations and societies.

The ninth and tenth commandments tell us not to even want what our neighbor has. If we lust after a neighbor's wife, the Lord tells us we have already committed adultery in our hearts (cf. Mt 5:28). If we envy others' possessions, we have already begun the act of stealing. Adultery and theft begin with unholy desire in the heart. They become acts of aggression when sinners place themselves above their neighbors and when their own desires become more important than their neighbors' rights. It is not evil to want what a neighbor has as long as it can be acquired justly, by gift or purchase. But a pure desire for our neighbor's goods can never be obsessive. Clearly, obedience to these commandments—and to all God's commandments—requires a true on-going conversion of the heart.

The *Catechism* reminds us that the "heart" is the seat of moral personality. "The struggle against carnal covetousness entails purifying the heart and practicing temperance." To be pure in heart "refers to those who have attuned their intellects and wills to the demands of God's holiness, chiefly in three areas: charity; chastity or sexual rectitude; love of truth and orthodoxy of faith" (nos. 2517-2518).

Quoting St. Augustine, the *Catechism* tells us:

> The faithful must believe the articles of the Creed "so that by believing they may obey God, by obeying may live well, by living well may purify their hearts, and with pure hearts may understand what they believe."
>
> Purity of heart is the precondition of the vision of God. Even now it enables us to see *according to* God, to accept others as "neighbors"; it lets us perceive the human body—ours and our neighbor's—as a temple of the Holy Spirit, a manifestation of divine beauty (nos. 2518-2519).

For a more complete study of these commandments, please refer to the *Catechism*. No Catholic home or office should be without this wonderful resource. Its contents are the authentic teachings of the Church.

Reflection:

- "Justice" is a constant concern in Church and in the world. As Catholics, what might we do to help people better understand the meaning of justice?
- Name some ways in which stealing seems acceptable among certain groups of people.
- What might motivate a person to steal? Is stealing ever justified?
- In what ways do people covet their neighbor's spouse? Why is this harmful?

Chapter 23

Do Not Lie about Your Neighbor

An employer who was widely known, respected and admired had a terribly low self image and needed constant affirmation despite his many gifts, talents and achievements. That need for affirmation led him to surround himself with "yes men." These favored employees consistently built up their boss's ego and told him he was the best in his field. The employer became very prideful. In his pride, he grew ruthless in his struggle for excellence, profit and prestige. He used and discarded people at whim.

At last, even the favored employees regarded him as a heartless monster whose facility at charming people was an evil in itself. However, for fear of losing their own jobs, they continued to build up their boss through adulation and flattery. No one had the courage to tell him the truth. No one loved him enough to tell him the truth.

Movies and soap operas thrive on such fare. Unfortunately, such a scenario is all too common in daily life. In business, education, family and parish life, the danger always lurks that people will offend truth by aiding and abetting a person who is living a lie, or even worse, propagating untruth as truth.

"You shall not bear false witness against your neighbor." In the above story, the fearful employees were indeed bearing false witness since they encouraged the lie their employer was living. They confirmed their boss's usury of fellow employees, thereby affirming the lie that an employee is mere chattel; they subordinated the truths revealed by God to their own needs which fear exacerbated.

It is too easy to say, "I do not offend the eighth commandment because I do not lie under oath." The commandments are the foundation upon which our entire moral system is built. Jesus revealed the height, breadth and depth of the commandments when he gave us the Beatitudes. We are blessed when we are pure of heart, strive for justice and peace, or mourn with Jesus for the souls of those who sin as a way of life.

According to the *Catechism of the Catholic Church*, we sin against the eighth commandment if we speak a falsehood publicly (cf. nos. 2475-2487). In court it is called false witness. If a lie is spoken under an oath to tell the truth it is called perjury.

> Acts such as these contribute to condemnation of the innocent, exoneration of the guilty, or the increased punishment of the accused. They gravely compromise the exercise of justice and the fairness of judicial decisions (no. 2476).

Although most of us never go to court, the eighth commandment covers all relationships in life. We must respect the reputation of others. We are guilty of *prejudice* and *rash judgment* when we easily assume the worst about others. We must not disclose the real faults of others without valid reason. For example, if employees suffer at the hands of an arrogant boss, they are not supposed to malign the employer and try to ruin his reputation. The Christian obligation is first to go to the employer and point out the faults. If that doesn't work, then the employees must find other charitable ways in which to address the problem, such as an appeal board. They would never be justified in gossiping privately or publicly about the boss.

Another example comes to mind about a Christian "healer" who had a ministry of prayer. People would confide very private matters to that person. The minister never actually revealed any "secrets" but had the habit of saying to common acquaintances: "Oh, by the way, please keep Susie in your prayers. She really has a very grave problem." Such a well-meaning request for prayer can easily start the rumor mill going!

A person is guilty of *calumny* when he or she lies about another, causing harm to that person's reputation and encouraging others to make false judgments.

It almost seems providential that the eighth commandment, which demands truth in charity for the sake of justice, ends this presentation of Church teaching on morality. Ample evidence shows that falsehood has become ingrained in our society. Citizens increasingly distrust their public officials and the news media, which is supposed to present factual information devoid of political or philosophical bias. We need only to see how shabbily the Church is often treated to realize how untrustworthy some media have become.

Entertainment passes off as normal the most immoral behavior—particularly on so-called radio and television "talk shows." In the minds of the stars, producers and commercial sponsors of these largely inane and limp excursions into the ridiculous, there are no moral norms rooted in immutable truth, that is, in the heart and mind of God.

Some lies are so subtle and have been "preached" for so long that society largely accepts them without challenge, for example, that lust is synonymous with love; mere desire, with real need; luxury, with necessity. Our society unashamedly embraces materialism as a way of life and personal gratification as its driving force. True, many exceptions exist, perhaps more than we realize. However, a study of how we express ourselves in entertainment and in public moral values gives rise to serious concern.

Then, in the Church itself, we find people embracing untruth in various ways. People do lie about others, ruin reputations, fire people unjustly, and flatter others to the point that pride and arrogance are more than temptations. In the Church, some people teach youngsters personal opinion rather than authentic truth as defined and taught by the Holy Father and the bishops. Still others, self-styled vigilantes for orthodoxy, flick their tongues with lies and half truths about priests, bishops and theologians, trying to pass off their own understanding of truth as *the truth* taught by Christ and his Church.

Jesus said in response to a question from Thomas: "I am the way, and the truth, and the life" (Jn 14:6). As he stood before Pilate, Jesus said: "Everyone who belongs to the truth listens to my voice." And we know Pilate's response: "What is truth?" (Jn 18:37b-38).

As the *Catechism* teaches:

> The disciple of Christ consents to "live in the truth," that is, in the simplicity of a life in conformity with the Lord's example, abiding in his truth. "If we say we have fellowship with him while we walk in darkness, we lie and do not live according to the truth" (no. 2470).

As Catholics we believe that Jesus founded our Church and gave Peter, the apostles and their successors the authority to interpret Scripture, to teach truth, to define doctrine and to guide and rule. Jesus promised to be with his Church always and to protect us against the "gates of hell" which would never defeat us.

The eighth commandment reminds us of the great value of truth. May God help us to live the Way, the Truth and the Life, under the guidance of our Holy Father and bishops, regardless of difficulties, dangers or popular opinion.

Reflection:

- Name some common ways in which people "bear false witness" against others.
- How does truth promote justice?
- Have you ever been a victim of gossip or calumny? If so, share with a friend how this affected you and how you resolved the situation. Or is it still unresolved? Why?

Books by Henry Libersat

Pauline Books & Media

Way, Truth and Life
Do Whatever He Tells You
A Catholic Confession of Faith
    Book One: *We Believe*
    Book Two: *We Celebrate the Mystery*
    Book Three: *We Live the Good Life*
    Book Four: *We Pray*

Servant Publications

Miracles Do Happen
(co-author for Sister Briege McKenna)

Godparents

Rekindle Your Life in the Spirit
(co-author with Babsie Bleasdell)

Pauline BOOKS & MEDIA

ALASKA
750 West 5th Ave., Anchorage, AK 99501; 907-272-8183

CALIFORNIA
3908 Sepulveda Blvd., Culver City, CA 90230; 310-397-8676
5945 Balboa Ave., San Diego, CA 92111; 619-565-9181
46 Geary Street, San Francisco, CA 94108; 415-781-5180

FLORIDA
145 S.W. 107th Ave., Miami, FL 33174; 305-559-6715

HAWAII
1143 Bishop Street, Honolulu, HI 96813; 808-521-2731

ILLINOIS
172 North Michigan Ave., Chicago, IL 60601; 312-346-4228

LOUISIANA
4403 Veterans Memorial Blvd., Metairie, LA 70006; 504-887-7631

MASSACHUSETTS
50 St. Paul's Ave., Jamaica Plain, Boston, MA 02130; 617-522-8911
Rte. 1, 885 Providence Hwy., Dedham, MA 02026; 617-326-5385

MISSOURI
9804 Watson Rd., St. Louis, MO 63126; 314-965-3512

NEW JERSEY
561 U.S. Route 1, Wick Plaza, Edison, NJ 08817; 908-572-1200

NEW YORK
150 East 52nd Street, New York, NY 10022; 212-754-1110
78 Fort Place, Staten Island, NY 10301; 718-447-5071

OHIO
2105 Ontario Street, Cleveland, OH 44115; 216-621-9427

PENNSYLVANIA
9171-A Roosevelt Blvd., Philadelphia, PA 19114; 215-676-9494

SOUTH CAROLINA
243 King Street, Charleston, SC 29401; 803-577-0175

TENNESSEE
4811 Poplar Ave., Memphis, TN 38117; 901-761-2987

TEXAS
114 Main Plaza, San Antonio, TX 78205; 210-224-8101

VIRGINIA
1025 King Street, Alexandria, VA 22314; 703-549-3806

CANADA
3022 Dufferin Street, Toronto, Ontario, Canada M6B 3T5; 416-781-9131
1155 Yonge Street, Toronto, Ontario, Canada M4T 1W2; 416-934-3440